Mary Moody's
ROSES

Mary Moody's
ROSES

More than 200 of the world's most beautiful and hardy roses

Mary Moody

MURDOCH BOOKS

Contents

Author's note

It is easy to be overwhelmed by the thousands of rose varieties available. Too much choice can lead to confusion, with gardeners scratching their heads in puzzlement about which rose is right for their climate, their soil and their garden design requirements. This book, I hope, will help to demystify the process of selecting the best roses for every possible purpose. The excellent photographs will help gardeners to choose their favourite flower form and colour, while the accompanying information about height, growth habit and specific health requirements will assist in narrowing down the field yet again. Ultimately, the choices you make should be based purely on the roses that most appeal to your senses. The colour, the form of the flower and the fragrance are factors that will pull at your heart strings and dictate which ones you wish to nurture in cultivation.

In my travels I have admired roses growing wild on rocky mountain hillsides in the Himalayas; in traditional gardens and public parks in China; in private gardens throughout England, Ireland and Wales; against stone walls in small villages in rural France; in famous French gardens such as the Bagatelle in Paris and Monet's garden at Giverny; in bustling New York and wind-swept Long Island; and in the rural gardens of outback Australia. In all these situations roses stand out for the sheer beauty of their blooms and their ability to somehow adapt and be at home in so many different landscapes.

Beside my front doorway in France is a thriving hybrid musk rose, smothered in small, pale pink flowers from late spring onwards. It cheers me to visit in the spring and watch it burst into life despite months and months of neglect.

Once you start on the rose-growing journey it becomes addictive. Each rose has its own particular charm and as flowering plants for gardens both large and small they are difficult to surpass. Their ease of cultivation and prolific flowering make them irresistible as cut flowers for the house and the recurrent flowering of many varieties makes them capable of being enjoyed from spring right through until autumn.

For the love of a rose

Without question, the rose is the world's most adored flowering plant. Although originally native only to the northern hemisphere, roses can now be found growing successfully in every corner of the globe, both in careful cultivation and also as wild plants, struggling to send roots down in rocky crevices on roadsides and sunny banks.

Indeed, no other flower in history has been hybridized as successfully and often as the rose, to the point now where there are hundreds of new varieties introduced every year. There are also those that are introduced, but remain popular for only a few seasons and then disappear. Just as fashion follows fads and trends, so do roses change from decade to decade, according to what types the breeders are producing and what types the gardening public is choosing to cultivate.

The rose is adored for many reasons, the main one being its stunning blooms. Many roses are also highly fragrant, in particular the old-fashioned varieties, and this adds greatly to their appeal. And finally, in spite of the fragility of the blooms, roses are extremely robust, easy-care plants that can survive quite tough growing conditions and a wide variety of soils, climates and conditions, making them popular with gardeners.

A long and tangled history

Evidence of the human attraction to roses has been recorded over thousands of years, with rose motifs decorating buildings in Assyria and Babylon. In Egyptian tombs dating back to the time of Alexander the Great, rose wreaths depicting the wild *Rosa gallica* were discovered and it is believed that during the time

The soft, velvety, red petals of 'Lady Brisbane' epitomize the appeal of the rose in colour, form and fragrance. Every year hundreds of new varieties are introduced worldwide.

of the famous Egyptian queen Cleopatra, roses were actually cultivated in the Nile Delta and exported to the upper classes in Rome to brighten their winter interiors. Images of roses can be seen in early Persian art, and they were also the flower associated with the legendary Aphrodite, the Greek goddess of love. Greek traders carried roses across Europe and to the Mediterranean islands, and in ancient Rome rose-growing areas were established in Campania for the cut-flower market.

For centuries roses were used as the basis of the perfume industry in France. In the thirteenth century, the highly fragrant *R. gallica* was mass-planted for this purpose. However it was not until the eighteenth century that the interest in breeding roses started in earnest, as plant explorers ventured into China in search of rose species that not only flowered right through the season, but also featured yellow petals, which were unheard of in the West.

Although some data has been lost in the mists of time, it is still possible to trace the history of the rose as we know it today, as so many varieties are interrelated, and all are ultimately descended from the wild or species roses.

Wild roses were the first roses identified and cultivated, and are the parents of all the roses we know today, and include such classics as the sweet briar rose (*Rosa eglanteria*), the dog rose (*Rosa canina*), the Scotch rose (*Rosa pimpinellifolia*) and the China rose (*Rosa chinensis*). Wild roses hail from the meadows of Britain, right across Europe and the Middle East to China and also the North American continent. The original wild roses were quite prickly shrubs or ramblers with simple blooms which generally flowered only once in the season. Over thousands of years roses naturally hybridized in the wild, producing new and interesting forms with single, semi-double or fully double flowers, in a large variety of colours from pure white through every shade of pink to deepest red. Wild roses are characterized by simple flowers with five petals and prominent yellow stamens. They are very vigorous and easy to grow, and often have a delightful fragrance.

Next came the gallica roses, starting with *Rosa gallica* – a small-growing, suckering rose from southern Europe with mid-green foliage and soft pink to red flowers.

In thirteenth-century France, the town of Provins, south of Paris, was famous for an industry based on the fantastic properties of *Rosa gallica officinalis* (the apothecary's rose). The Empress Josephine also used gallicas as the basis of her rose-breeding program, which is why so many wonderful gallicas date back to the early 1800s and have French names.

After gallicas came the damask roses, which had been cultivated since ancient times and are also descended from *Rosa gallica*. There are two forms: summer damasks that flower only once, and autumn damasks that flower again in autumn. They can grow to 2.5 m (8 ft), according to the variety, and they have wonderfully scented clusters of flowers in the white, pink and red colour range.

Another ancient group is the alba roses, which are thought to be a cross between the dog rose (*Rosa canina*) and *Rosa gallica*. They are very fragrant with foliage that has a distinctive bluish tinge, and the flowers are always either white or palest pink. In time they develop into a lovely dense shrub, covered with flowers in early summer. They have very few thorns, which is a bonus for some gardeners.

Admired for their prickly stems are the moss roses, which were first recorded in the early eighteenth century as sports or mutations on various roses such as centifolias or damasks, and from these unusual stems many varieties were bred. The name 'moss' comes from the unusual mossy green sepals that cover the flower buds, which is a unique feature.

OPPOSITE Wild roses, such as *Rosa moyesii* were brought from China and introduced to eager gardeners in the West during the eighteenth and nineteenth centuries. Over time the wild roses were used to breed modern varieties, such as the dainty miniature rose 'Gourmet Popcorn', pictured here.

Also popular are the centifolia roses, sometimes known as cabbage roses. They first appeared in the sixteenth century, and were a cross between the autumn damask and an alba rose. They are wonderful, floppy bushes with huge, fragrant flowers that hang on rather slim stems – it was roses like this that later encouraged breeders to develop the stiff, upright stems of the hybrid tea roses. One of the best centifolias is 'Fantin-Latour', which has numerous pink petals that curve inwards, hiding the centre.

Not as prevalent are the Portland roses, named after the Duchess of Portland, and first recognized in 1792 as a hybrid between the autumn damask and *Rosa gallica officinalis*. They are adored for their rich red or pink flowers and wonderful form.

The Chinese had bred roses for centuries before they were discovered by the plant-hunters and introduced to Europe. These plant-hunters were intrepid botanical explorers who infiltrated countries including China, Tibet, Nepal, Turkey and Southeast Asia to collect and transport plant material back to the Western world. The roses they brought from China caused a revolution in the rose-breeding world as they flowered right through the season, rather than having just one flush of blooms in early summer. The original China roses were small shrubs, growing to about 1 m (3 ft), with red or pink, single or loosely double blooms.

Also from China came the original tea rose (*Rosa* x *odorata*), which is a hybrid between *Rosa gigantea* and *Rosa chinensis*, and they were much admired in China before the famous 'Humes Blush' tea-scented China

rose was taken to Europe in 1809. Tea roses are either small bushes or climbers with flowers in the pink, buff or pale yellow colour range. From these Chinese imports many wonderful varieties are descended, including bourbon roses, which are believed to be a natural hybrid between *Rosa chinensis* and the autumn damask – apparently they had been grown together as a hedge and produced offspring with bright pink, scented flowers. The seeds of this rose were sent to France in 1820 and crossed with various gallica and damask hybrids to produce a delightful range of roses.

During the time of Napoleon, the Empress Josephine was a great rose enthusiast, commissioning plant-hunters to collect rare wild species and hybrids from all over the world and growing them in profusion around Malmaison, her grand country estate near Paris. The botanical artist Pierre Joseph Redouté painted Josephine's favourite rose varieties at Malmaison, and his works were published in 1817. They remain to this day the most famous and best-loved paintings of classical roses.

The allure of rose breeding spread through the New World, resulting in delightful discoveries such as the noisette roses, which were first bred in the United States. These old roses are a hybrid between *Rosa moschata* and 'Parson's Pink China', a climber with delightful clusters of semi-double pink flowers. In time they were crossbred with 'Park's Yellow China' to produce a range of large-flowered climbers.

Also of interest are the hybrid perpetual roses, which were hybrids between the Portland rose and a China hybrid. These were very popular in the latter part of the nineteenth century, with literally thousands of varieties being bred, of which less than one hundred survive today. They are characterized by very large

OPPOSITE (CLOCKWISE FROM TOP LEFT) 'Charles de Mills' (gallica rose), 'Vienna Charm' (hybrid tea rose), 'William Shakespeare' (David Austin English rose) and 'Circus' (floribunda rose).

flowers in the white, pink, mauve and red colour range and they are very vigorous growers in a wide range of soils and climates.

Another beautiful group is the hybrid musk roses. These are tall, recurrent-flowering, scented roses that were first bred in Britain at the beginning of the twentieth century. This group includes several excellent varieties, including 'Felicia' and 'Penelope', that date from the 1920s.

Never to be forgotten are the charming rugosa roses, which usually (but not always) have dark green, crinkly leaves and large flowers in the white, pink and red colour range, and there are also some yellow-flowering hybrids. They are very tough and hardy, hailing from northern Japan and Korea, usually with spiny stems and showy rosehips that follow the flowers. They seem to resist black spot and other fungal diseases, and don't need much care and attention. They are delightful all year round.

However, during recent times, it is the hybrid tea roses that have become the most popular group. These were the result of combining tea roses with hybrid perpetuals to create a rose which featured the elegance of the tea roses and the robustness and recurrent flowering of the hybrid perpetuals.

Another popular group is the floribunda roses, also known as 'cluster-flowered' roses, because they carry large numbers of blooms on each stem.

Also popular are the modern English roses bred by David Austin. These are shrub roses that carry many of the characteristics of old roses, including fragrance, but flower continuously through the season in a wide range of colours from snowy white through all the yellows to pinks and deepest reds.

The story of this evolution brings us right up to today. However, as botanical geneticists become more adept at tracing the history of the rose using DNA studies, this history will no doubt become clearer and even more compelling.

Enduring appeal

Apart from their hardiness and adaptability to a wide range of soils and climates, roses have endured as favourites because of the comparative ease and success of their hybridization. After observing the accidental crosses in the wild, rose enthusiasts began to experiment with blending different colours and forms to produce 'improved' strains for eager gardeners all around the world. The most profound development came after the introduction of the recurrent-flowering roses from China, which changed the nature of roses in cultivation from being plants that burst into flower for only a few short weeks every year. Suddenly it became possible to breed roses that would flower, more or less continuously, from spring to autumn.

More recently the development of the hybrid tea rose, which concentrated on developing the perfect high-centred flower form on long, strong stems for cutting, has changed the appearance of roses dramatically. In the process of breeding these specific characteristics, other appealing qualities, such as perfume, have been lost along the way. This is where David Austin has come to the fore, developing roses that have all the charm and softness of the old-fashioned favourites, combined with recurrent flowering and, in many cases, strong perfume.

OPPOSITE Although the formal flowers of hybrid tea roses are popular, gardeners are also seeking softer, more old-fashioned blooms such as 'Blossomtime', pictured here, with its muddled centres.

These days gardeners have the option of selecting from the most highly stylized designer roses for cutting and exhibition, to the simple, original wild roses of the field that are now widely available in nurseries and from mail order specialists. Roses can be used in so many ways around the garden – as hedges, climbers for covering trellises and archways, for mass-planting and as accent plants.

An old-fashioned revival

In the middle of the twentieth century serious breeding of roses was undertaken right around the world. In many ways it seems strange, given the huge number of species and natural hybrids that were available to rose growers, that there needed to be so many new roses developed. But the quest was always one for the 'perfect' rose – a rose that had excellent growth and vigour, high resistance to pest and disease infestations, improved colour, stronger stems for picking and for florists, increased numbers of blooms and improved overall effect. The popularity of the new improved varieties had the effect of reducing the sales of old-fashioned or species varieties in nurseries, and for many decades old roses were rarely seen.

While these new rose varieties were indeed highly decorative, many gardeners found them rather stiff and contrived – not soft and natural like their wild ancestors. As a result, in the 1980s there was a revival of interest in old roses, and gardeners began wanting to buy them and plant them once more. This consumer-led interest encouraged nurseries to start propagating the old varieties again and, within a few short years, several hundred long-forgotten roses were

OPPOSITE Climbing roses with an abundance of blooms, such as 'Edna Walling', pictured here, are stunning grown over an archway or through trellis.

A French damask rose dating back to 1845, 'Nuits de Young' has mossy stems and flowers that are considered to be the darkest red of all old roses.

once more available through rose specialist nurseries. Before long this trend hit the mainstream, and now there are very few worthwhile old rose varieties that are not available somewhere.

Most people like to grow a combination of old and new. And they do work well together because the newer roses are often better for picking, while the older-style roses look wonderful if left flowering on the plant. Also, in many situations old roses are less susceptible to pest and disease infestations (especially some of the rugosa roses, which seem impervious to black spot) and they require much less pruning and attention than their more modern counterparts. They also seem to need less feeding and watering to produce a wonderful display of blooms. These qualities have assured their ongoing appeal.

Rose culture

Despite the delicacy of their blooms, roses are real survivors. However, there is a vast difference between a rose that is simply 'surviving' in tough growing conditions, and one that has been given some extra care. Even though it is not uncommon to see neglected roses struggling and succeeding to produce flowers without adequate water or nutrients, the simple truth is that the same plant will do brilliantly if the growing environment is improved.

The soil

Roses prefer soil that has a capacity to hold moisture, but is still sufficiently well drained so that their root system won't become waterlogged. This means that gardens with heavy clay soil or light, sandy soil require some work to create the optimum growing conditions. This doesn't mean that the soil structure over the entire garden will require amendment. Simply providing some organic material around the roots of the rose at planting time is enough.

Clay soils

If drainage is very bad because of a heavy clay subsoil, it is advisable to create raised beds filled with a lighter and more friable soil, so that excess water can run away from the roots. Otherwise, simply incorporating a bag of well-rotted animal manure or a barrowload of homemade compost to open out the soil and create a better growing environment will do the trick.

Sandy soil

The main problem with sandy soils is that the nutrients immediately leach from the soil after rainfall or watering, and then soil then dries out. Once again

One of the great joys of growing roses is picking them for the house. Indeed, regular cutting of roses is an excellent way of stimulating new growth and promoting healthy, more robust bushes.

organic matter is the key to success. By simply bulking up the soil with bags or barrowloads of well-rotted manures and composts, the soil will be capable of holding moisture for longer periods, and in turn will then supply nutrients adequately to the roses.

Position

For maximum flowering roses need at least 5 or 6 hours of direct sunlight every day. Some gardeners get away with 4 hours of sun, and although it is possible to grow roses in areas of the garden that are even more shaded than that, the results will never be as spectacular. There are also some roses that can tolerate less sun, as they have been bred from wild roses that grew naturally in dappled woodland shade, but these are few and far between.

Gardeners with little or no sun can get around this problem to some extent by growing dwarf or miniature roses in pots or tubs that can be moved to sunny positions as the seasons change. However, gardens that are totally overshadowed by buildings or established trees are generally considered unsuitable.

When choosing a position for a rose bed look for an open area that is well away from large trees with invasive root systems that will compete for moisture and nutrients. Even if the area is sunny, the constant battle of keeping the roots out of the garden will be more trouble than it is worth. Also avoid areas that are prone to waterlogging or flooding.

Preparing the way

When a suitable location has been found prepare the ground by clearing it of weeds, rubble and lawn, then turn it over to a depth of at least 45 cm (1½ ft), lightly breaking up the ground to aerate it and make the soil friable. Prior to planting, dig in some good-quality organic matter – well-rotted cow manure or your own homemade compost. There should be no need to fertilize freshly planted roses – indeed it can cause root damage by burning the fine fibrous roots. Wait until the roses are growing well, then fertilize using a slow-release, organic plant food.

The most economical way of buying roses is during their dormant period in midwinter when they are sold bare-rooted (without soil around their root systems). There is a much wider selection of rose varieties sold this way and they are available at nurseries or garden centres and also via mail order. Make sure the rose will be the right size, shape and colour for your requirements. Always look for vigorous roses with strong stems and healthy leaf growth. Avoid plants that appear to have been damaged, with stems

Weed alert

Take care if buying bulk manures that they are well rotted, or you risk an invasion of weeds that can germinate once the manure is spread around the base of the roses. If uncertain, mix the manure with a couple of bales of old lucerne hay and leave it to break down for several weeks before applying it as a mulch. The heat generated in the rotting pile should hopefully destroy the viability of any weed seeds.

broken off or with yellowing foliage. Look at the rose from every angle to make sure it has a good all-round shape and that it is not lopsided or unevenly pruned. If you notice signs of black spot – yellowing and spotting of the foliage – avoid this variety, as it will probably cause you never-ending problems.

Planting out

Try and plant your container-grown or bare-rooted roses as quickly as possible when you get them home from the nursery. If they must sit around for a few days, keep them in the shade and well watered, then plant them out in the early evening, watering them in well. Bare-rooted roses benefit from sitting in a bucket of water with a few capfuls of liquid seaweed mix incorporated, for at least 1 hour prior to planting. Roses shouldn't require staking, unless they are standard varieties, and they should always be planted at the same level as in the container – don't bury the stem beneath ground level, as this will cause fungal problems and suckering.

Keeping roses healthy

Once established, roses will continue to grow quite vigorously no matter how harsh the environment. However if you follow a few basic routine

Climbing roses look glorious once they have become established. After planting, simply allow the long stems to grow unchecked, so they can twine around the support structure while they are young and pliable.

maintenance tasks the plants will be much less susceptible to pest and disease problems, and they will produce more prolific blooms for a longer period. Having healthy, glossy green foliage adds greatly to the charm of roses, even when they are not in flower. This means avoiding the various fungal diseases that plague rose growers everywhere.

Routine watering

Roses do not enjoy long, dry periods without rain or watering except in winter when their growth is dormant. From spring until late autumn, they need two long, deep soakings per week – obviously less during rainy periods. The best time to water roses is in the morning, because the sun will help to dry out the humidity – watering in the evening means the bushes

remain damp overnight, which only encourages fungal spores (the main cause of the problematic foliage disease known as black spot). The best idea is to water plants at ground level, thus avoiding splashing any moisture onto the foliage and flowers. The aim is to keep the bush itself dry, and the roots and soil nice and moist. Shallow watering is not advised because it encourages the roots of the plants to remain close to the surface. Deep watering has the effect of getting those roots down deep into the soil, making the plants stronger and more robust.

Effective mulching

Roses respond well to a good, deep layer of organic mulch around the base from early spring until late autumn. In winter, however, the mulch can be removed to allow the sun to warm the soil more easily. The most effective mulches for roses are those that supply nutrients as well as insulation, such as lucerne mulch, stable sweepings of horse manure and straw. However, they must be well rotted so, if uncertain, allow the bags to rot down for at least 4 weeks.

Mulching is highly recommended because it improves the growing environment. In spring and summer it helps to reduce water consumption by preventing the soil from drying out too quickly after watering. Mulches also improve the texture of the soil as they break down, helping it to be more free-draining, while also capable of holding moisture for longer periods.

As an added benefit, mulching suppresses weed growth, which is very important for roses because they resent competing with weeds or grass for moisture and nutrients, and because the weeds themselves create high levels of humidity at ground level which in turn can cause black spot.

The best time to start mulching is in early spring, to a depth of 8–10 cm (3–4 in), taking care not to pile the mulch up against the base of the plant, as this will cause humidity. Allow a little breathing space between the main stem and the mulch, and then top up the layer during the season if necessary.

Fertilizing regimes
Roses are sometimes referred to as 'greedy feeders', which simply means that they are fast-growing and prolific-flowering so they need plenty of boosting with nutrients to produce great results. Professional rose growers have a strict feeding regime, alternating between specially formulated fertilizers and various blends of manure that they use as mulch over the soil surface. For home gardeners it is just a matter of giving roses a steady supply of nutrients over spring, summer and early autumn.

Rose fertilizer must contain a balance of the essential nutrients (nitrogen, phosphorus and potassium) to produce lush foliage and flowers and, ideally, the plants should be fed with a combination – well-rotted manure mulch in early spring, followed by a specially formulated rose fertilizer (follow the manufacturer's advice on quantities). Feed again in early summer to maintain strong growth, then once again in late summer to boost the second flush of flowers in autumn.

Fungal problems
Black spot is a fungal disease that weakens plants and causes roses to shed their foliage, thus reducing vigour and flower production. The main symptoms are when the foliage starts to yellow and is covered with the characteristic black spots that give the disease its

The Meilland family have been breeding roses for generations, initially in northern France but now in the sunny south. This variety, 'Michèle Meilland', dates back to 1945.

Popularly known as the 'Yellow Rose of Texas', *Rosa x harisonii* was developed in the 1830s in the United States, and is still widely cultivated to this day.

common name. Black spot is probably the main problem experienced by keen rose growers, except for those fortunate enough to garden in hot, dry climates.

Prevention is the key to coping with this irritating disease. In winter, immediately after you have pruned your roses, dispose of all the fallen foliage and any stems or prunings on the ground – the spores of black spot lurk around over winter in rotting material. While the plants are still dormant (without any foliage) you can spray them and the soil around them with lime sulphur to completely destroy fungal spores, but take care, as this treatment can damage plants if applied when buds are forming or when early leaves appear. It should really only be done on leafless plants in winter.

In humid climates, regular sprays with a fungicide may be necessary. This should be done at 3-weekly intervals from the first appearance of foliage in spring. You may even need to use anti-fungal sprays weekly.

In areas where black spot is only a problem after heavy rain or later in the season, restrict spraying to these times, or if yellowing or spotted foliage is detected. Strike fast for immediate results.

Generally, at the first sign of foliage damage, pick off and destroy affected leaves. This reduces the rapid spread of the disease.

Aphid control

Aphids are tiny, sap-sucking insects that can be a real nuisance during a vital time in the growth cycle of the rose – the formation of the flower buds. Aphids will quickly smother an entire stem and bud, ruining it before it has a chance to open. Depending on the severity of the infestation, aphids can be controlled by manual removal (simply run your fingers up the stem and over the bud, squashing the insects), or by hosing them off with a strong spray of water. The danger, if you spray chemicals or even a natural insecticide such as pyrethrum, is that you will also kill valuable, predatory insects such as ladybirds, which feast on the aphids in large numbers. Birds are also a good way of keeping aphid populations down, and they should be encouraged into the garden with bird baths or nectar-producing plants.

Other problems

Roses are also affected by other problems that may need to be dealt with during the growing season.
- Powdery mildew: appears as a white coating on the foliage. A fungicide, like the one used against black spot, is the solution.
- Thrips: almost invisible insects that attack buds in some seasons. A harsh water spray will help, or chemical control using an insecticide.
- Two-spotted mite: bronze mottling and flecking of foliage. Release predatory mites that are available from integrated pest management organizations.

Pruning techniques

Some rose growers claim you can prune with a chain saw. However, more reliable results can be achieved with a gentler approach. Bush roses should be pruned when they are dormant in midwinter, or slightly later in cool to cold climates, to prevent a sudden burst of new growth that can be killed by frost.

Wear gloves and use clean, sharp pruning tools that have been given a wipe over with a cloth soaked in teatree oil or an all-purpose disinfectant. The aim is to concentrate growth while creating an open shape that allows good air and light circulation. Reduce the top of the bush by at least 50 per cent. Cut each limb to an outward-facing bud, cutting at a 45-degree angle that slants away from the bud (to prevent water collecting in the cut). Remove any dead or damaged stems, and also any weak or spindly stems. Prune again in late summer to encourage a second burst of flowers. This should be a lighter pruning, and plants should be fed at the same time.

Pruning climbing roses

Climbing and rambling roses require a totally different pruning approach, which again varies considerably according to the variety and its growth habit. After planting, the main aim with climbers is to allow those long stems to grow unimpeded for at least 2 years – while these fast-growing stems are young and pliable

Banana skins

Rose plants respond well to the potassium contained in banana skins, which can be used as mulch around the base. They look rather unsightly, but if covered with a scattering of leaves or lucerne straw, they will quickly rot down out of sight and your roses will benefit tremendously.

they can be trained to twine through trellis or over archways. As they grow, the climbing stems produce side shoots and these are the parts of the plant that can be pruned back at a later stage. On established stems the side shoots can be pruned back leaving two nodes – this concentrates the flowering. Most climbers are best pruned back after flowering – in many instances they will produce a second or even a third flush of blooms. Ramblers have more erratic and bushy growth than climbers, and are really only suited to large gardens where they can be allowed to grow without restriction. If you do grow a rambler in a smaller garden it will need to be trimmed back hard after flowering, simply to keep its size under control.

Pick those blooms

It can be heart-wrenching to pick roses when they are looking so wonderful on the plant. However, keep in mind that routine picking of the blooms is a great way to get even more blooms. Cut the stems as long as possible, to within three or four leaves of the stem's junction with the branch. This also helps to keep the plants more compact. Always pick roses in the early morning, looking for those that are just starting to open rather than those that are full blown.

Deadheading

If you have resisted the temptation to pick your roses, you will still need to remove the flowering stems once the petals have faded and fallen. This process is called deadheading and it is important, not only because it helps to keep the plant looking neat and tidy, but because it helps to concentrate growth and encourages further production of flowers. Every day when you are walking in the garden, simply cut off the spent flower stems and take them away for composting. Never allow them to just fall to the ground as this encourages fungal problems.

Designing with roses

Roses can be quite tricky to work into a well-designed landscape because they do not necessarily look beautiful all year round. During the winter months, when they have dropped their foliage and remain unpruned after the autumn flush, they can look very unsightly indeed. Therefore, positioning them where they will not be an eyesore during this period is quite a challenge for gardeners.

The old-fashioned notion was to grow roses on their own, in special beds that were generally plonked in the middle of the lawn, with wooden stakes to support the rose bushes, and lots of exposed, bare earth at ground level. This is no longer considered an option because the beds looks stark in winter and, despite the beauty of the flowers in summer, standing alone does not set them off to their best advantage.

Ideally shrub and standard roses should be planted in beds and borders surrounded by other foliage and flowering plants that highlight the beauty of their flowers. Climbing and rambling roses need to be given some sort of support – a trellis or climbing pole or fence where they can add height and drama to the landscape. In both situations the plants that are combined with roses should be selected not just for their complementary flower colours, but for their growth habit. Rampant shrubs and perennials that crowd the bases of the roses are not really suitable, because they create humidity which in turn sets off fungal diseases, especially black spot. Low-growing, trailing plants that allow good air circulation around your roses will create a lovely visual framework without causing disease problems.

Plants to avoid

Avoid planting roses directly into the lawn – even though this is a popular practice in Europe, it really means that you will be feeding and spraying your roses constantly to keep them looking good. Lawn competes with roses for moisture and nutrients and lawn grasses with invasive roots will smother the fine feeder roots of the roses. The lawnmower will also damage the roses, breaking off stems and leaving them open for infection.

Never plant roses near acacias, because the sweet sticky sap of those plants is a breeding ground for fungal diseases that can quickly spread into your rose plants. Likewise, tall-growing plants will produce too much ground-level moisture that creates the ideal environment for black spot, so avoid these too.

Most Australian native plant species dislike the rich nutrients required in a rose garden, and they definitely resent the lime and phosphorus in rose fertilizer.

Visually, you should avoid other plants with bright, glossy green foliage because they will look too similar and the roses will be lost in the scheme of things – instead, look for plants with silver or burgundy or pale lime green foliage that will really make the roses leap out and shout for attention.

Good companions

There are many plants that are perfect companions for roses, both for visual reasons and disease-prevention purposes. From a purely symbiotic point of view, elderberry seems to have a beneficial effect on roses.

Vita Sackville-West's famous white garden, at Sissinghurst in England, features a dramatic arbour, smothered in the rampant old climber *Rosa longicuspis* that has clusters of small, white, fragrant blooms.

It is thought that the foliage of the elderberry has fungicidal properties, therefore it probably exudes these essences into the atmosphere, reducing fungal problems on nearby plants.

Members of the onion family, such as chives, garlic, leeks, onions and shallots, are excellent companions to plant with roses because they send out a strong aroma that repels insects and, if regularly cut, also help to prevent diseases such as black spot and mildew. Rose growers have reported varying success using this method, and seem to think that garlic is the most effective of all. The appearance of the companion plant will be the deciding factor here.

Other herbs worth considering as companion plants to roses are mints, which are said to repel insects and make good groundcovers. Ginger mint is said to be the most effective. The mint family is also good at repelling earwigs, which can be a real problem in some gardens. The foliage is also complementary to the foliage of the roses.

Common marjoram is a good groundcover with golden foliage that is very complementary. Coriander will help to repel aphids (as will dwarf nasturtiums, dwarf marigolds, parsley and pyrethrum daisies).

Lavender, especially dwarf lavender, is a fantastic companion for many reasons. It has soft grey-green foliage which complements the glossy green foliage of the roses, and it doesn't grow too tall. Lavender oil is a mild fungicide, therefore it is also reputed to be a good prevention for black spot. The foliage of the lavender isn't too thick, and therefore it also won't create too much ground-level moisture. The dwarf lavender mostly hightly recommended by English rose growers is the variety 'Munstead'.

Good old-fashioned pelargoniums (commonly called geraniums – but not to be confused with the cranesbills which are the real geranium species) are also good companions for roses. The scented varieties are good insect repellents, discouraging the leaf-eating beetles that can sometimes attack roses. Most species and varieties appreciate a good heavy pruning, and therefore can be kept growing low around the base of the plants. There are also small-leafed varieties which will remain quite compact and not grow too tall. The only disadvantage may be that the fragrance of the pelargoniums may clash with the fragrance of any highly scented roses.

Contrasting colours

Soft grey-green or silver foliage plants are an excellent visual foil for roses. Lamb's ears (*Stachys* sp.) looks wonderful, and can be trimmed back if the flower stems start growing too tall, depending on the rose variety. However, keep it from growing too close to the base of the rose. Easy to propagate by division, many species of lamb's ears also self-seed easily, and can be potted up and given to friends or spread around the garden.

Nepeta sp. (catmint) is also ideal, with grey foliage and lavender-blue flowers. A lot of keen rose growers use it as a border around the edge of the rose garden and, because it is a perennial, it will grow and last for years and years. Another excellent grey foliage plant is santolina, which has yellow flowers and looks very pretty with cream or yellow roses (but not pink).

As a complete contrast in foliage colour, try the bronzy-red shrub *Berberis thunbergii* 'Atropurpurea Nana'. It is low growing and looks particularly effective with white, pink and deep red roses.

The famous rose arches in Monet's French garden lead from the bottom of the garden to the front door of his house. Each arch is planted with different coloured climbers that are carefully trained to meet in the middle.

Carpeting and groundcovering plants are excellent around roses, as they keep lawn and weeds out of the garden. Consider a carpet of chamomile as a soil surface insulator – it is also reputed to complement the fragrance of some roses, making them smell sweeter.

There is a range of interesting and colourful perennials that are very effective because many have basically the same requirements as roses – full sun and rich, well-drained but still moist soil. Consider the following: *Alchemilla mollis* with wonderful foliage that holds droplets of water, and greenish yellow flowers; *Alyssum saxatile* with greyish foliage and yellow flowers; some of the lower-growing euphorbias; aquilegias (columbines); cranesbills (geraniums); sedums (fleshy, almost succulents); campanula (the lower-growing varieties with blue flowers); artemisias (again with silver foliage, keep them clipped low) and rudbeckia, which is great with yellow or orange roses.

Annuals are terrific as long as you don't dig up the soil around the base of the roses too much when planting them. They provide a good splash of colour to fill in during those periods when the roses are not flowering. Try the following: primulas which are good for an early colour display; lobelia, which is good as it has a spreading, carpeting habit and some varieties have bronze-green foliage; alyssum, especially the cream-flowering variety; the dwarf variety of nasturtiums, because they are good insect repellents – just be careful that their strong flower colours don't clash with the roses; forget-me-nots are gorgeous under roses, but remember that after one season you will have them everywhere in the garden – be prepared for a total invasion; violets and pansies look charming, especially with old-fashioned roses; and if the garden has space for background plants consider lupins, foxgloves and hollyhocks which are delightful.

The Meilland-bred 'Charles de Gaulle' is a hybrid tea rose from the 1970s, still popular for its sweetly scented and perfectly formed, clear pink flowers.

Spring-flowering bulbs, such as daffodils, tulips and jonquils in particular, are great when they have become established, and will provide colour before the roses come into their own. Also consider growing snowdrops, crocuses, grape hyacinths and spring star flowers (*Ipheon* sp.). The beauty of the bulbs is that they often flower early, bringing colour to the garden before the dormant rose stems start coming into leaf. They can be overplanted with annuals that will grow up as the weather warms, covering the spent flower stems and foliage of the bulbs which must be allowed to die back naturally.

Whatever plants you choose to grow with your roses, be prepared to change things around if the effect doesn't work or if you get bored with it. Gardens should be every changing and evolving – never static – and it is fun to experiment with different plant combinations and colour schemes to keep your garden landscape interesting.

WILD
ROSES

The earliest recorded roses are the wild, or species, roses of the field and roadside. Native to the northern hemisphere, wild roses were seen from ancient times, growing right across Europe, the Middle East, China and North America in a wide variety of climates and situations. There are still wild roses growing down grassy banks in France and England, and rampant, wild climbing roses smothering treetops in the Indian Himalayas.

Wild roses are distinguished by their simplicity, often having single, five-petalled flower forms, colourful seed-bearing rosehips and untamed growth habits. In the wild these roses provide a habitat for birds and insects, and they can perform the same valuable function in domestic gardens. Included in this category are several hybrid forms of wild roses that have been derived from the parent plant and have often become more popular with modern gardeners. Wild roses are often scented and are generally easier to grow than many of their modern counterparts, having adapted to rough growing conditions and poorer soils. They can sometimes be grown in semi-shaded situations.

PREVIOUS PAGE *Rosa foetida persiana*

R. banksiae alba plena

History: A handsome climbing shrub rose discovered in Canton, China, in 1807, it was transported to Britain by the plant explorer William Kerr. It was known as Lady Banks' rose, in honour of the wife of Sir Joseph Banks, the director of Kew Gardens at that time.

Description: This is the double, white-flowering form of the banksia rose. It has dense, shrubby growth but throws out tall, arching canes that can reach 6 m (20 ft) or more in height if the rose is planted in the right situation. The foliage is light green and glossy, and the small white flowers are carried in clusters from late spring into early summer and are highly fragrant. Like most banksia roses it has virtually no thorns.

Parentage: Unknown

Other names: Double white banksian rose, 'Lady Banks'

Suggested usage: The fast and dense growth of this rose makes it ideal for hedging and screening and for hiding unsightly walls or garden buildings. In smaller gardens, prune it back regularly to check the rampant growth.

■ FLOWERS ONCE ONLY
▨ FULL SUN
■ RELATIVELY DISEASE-FREE

R. banksiae fortuniana

History: A hybrid of two wild roses not actually seen growing in the wild, it was introduced to Britain in 1850.

Description: A handsome climbing shrub rose with deeper green stems and foliage than other banksia roses. The flowers are large, double and pure white in colour with a delightful fragrance, and appear in spring and early summer. This rose grows to 3.5 m (11½ ft), spreading to 2.5 m (8 ft), and responds to light pruning in late summer.

Parentage: Presumed hybrid between *R. banksiae* and *R. laevigata*

Other names: None

Suggested usage: A more tender rose than some, it needs protection from very cold or windy weather. It makes a good hedging rose in a sheltered situation, with attractive foliage long after the flowers have finished.

▨ FLOWERS ONCE ONLY
▨ FULL SUN
▨ RELATIVELY DISEASE-FREE

R. canina

History: This ancient wild rose is the most common species seen naturalized throughout Britain and Europe.

Description: A dense, prickly shrub rose that grows to 5 m (16½ ft), *R. canina* is extremely tough and vigorous. The stems are reddish and the foliage is small and mid-green in colour. The abundant, sweetly scented flowers are small and charming, with single blooms that range in colour from white to pale pink with rich yellow stamens. The spring to summer flowers are followed in late summer and autumn by small, orange-red hips that are a rich source of vitamin C. There are at least sixty forms and hybrids of *R. canina*.

Parentage: Unknown

Other names: Dog rose

Suggested usage: This is a charming rose for semi-shaded woodland gardens. It is tolerant of even quite poor soils and less-than-perfect growing conditions.

▨ FLOWERS ONCE ONLY
▨ FULL SUN TO SEMI-SHADE
▨ DISEASE-RESISTANT

R. x dupontii

History: A wild European rose that was a natural hybrid identified by plant explorers sometime prior to 1817.

Description: This is a strong-growing, shrubby rose that can reach 1.8 m (6 ft) in height with pale green, slender stems and a good covering of greyish green foliage. The open, single flowers are white with a pale pink flush near the edge, and have a beautiful shape, with prominent yellow stamens at their centre. The flowers appear somewhat later in the season than most non-recurrent roses, and in turn the hips tend not to appear until late in autumn. The flowers have a delightful, sweet fragrance.

Parentage: Possibly *R. gallica* x *R. moschata*

Other names: Dupont rose, snow-bush rose

Suggested usage: This is a very decorative shrub rose due to its outstanding white blooms. Use it as the centrepiece of a white-themed garden bed, or as a background rose in a mixed border. It is also sometimes used as a hedging shrub.

■ FLOWERS ONCE ONLY
■ FULL SUN
■ DISEASE-RESISTANT

R. ecae 'Golden Chersonese'

History: A hybrid of the wild form *R. ecae*, developed by English breeder E. F. Allen in 1963. The parent species is native to Afghanistan and was discovered in 1880.

Description: A handsome bushy shrub rose, growing to 1.8 m (6 ft), it has deep brown, thorny stems and prolific, rich green, ferny foliage. The flowers are abundant and bloom quite early in the season from mid- to late spring, before many other roses come into flower. The flowers are single with five petals in a rich shade of golden-yellow, also with golden-yellow stamens.

Parentage: A hybrid of *R. ecae* and 'Canary Bird'

Other names: None

Suggested usage: This shrubby rose can be pruned to make a robust specimen shrub in a mixed flower bed or border. As it is one of the few roses that can tolerate poorer soils and shade, it makes a good woodland planting – obviously it will flower better the more sun it gets each day.

- FLOWERS ONCE ONLY
- FULL SUN TO SEMI-SHADE
- DISEASE-RESISTANT

R. fedtschenkoana

History: A suckering shrub native to Central Asia and China, introduced to the West at the end of the nineteenth century.

Description: This is an unusual but highly attractive shrub rose with pale grey-green, feathery foliage. Its vigorous upright growth of prickly stems can reach 2 m (6½ ft) in height, and the single white flowers have fine, papery petals and prominent yellow stamens. Although the flowering season is early and abundant this rose will spot-flower right through the season before producing clusters of decorative, pear-shaped, orange-red hips. The flowers are fragrant, but to many the scent is unappealing.

Parentage: Unknown

Other names: None

Suggested usage: This is a useful specimen shrub because of its unusual overall appearance. It makes a fine hedging rose and can also tolerate poorer soils and some shade, making it suitable for a woodland planting.

- ■ RECURRENT-FLOWERING
- ■ FULL SUN TO SEMI-SHADE
- ■ DISEASE-RESISTANT

R. filipes 'Kiftsgate'

History: A hybrid of the wild climber R. filipes, developed at Kiftsgate Court in Gloucestershire, England, in 1954. The parent species is a native of western China.

Description: One of the largest-growing and most vigorous climbing roses in the world, 'Kiftsgate' can reach 10.5 m (34½ ft) in height, clambering up and over mature trees and generally smothering all in its path. It has small but wonderfully fragrant, creamy white single flowers followed by tiny, decorative red hips in late summer. The foliage is particularly glossy and green, colouring to russet-red in autumn, making it ornamental even when not in flower.

Parentage: Sport of R. filipes

Other names: None

Suggested usage: In large gardens this rose is ideal for covering unsightly fences or outbuildings, or for running up into trees. It is also perfect for climbing over a sturdy pergola.

- ■ FLOWERS ONCE ONLY
- ■ TOLERATES SOME SHADE
- ■ DISEASE-RESISTANT

R. foetida bicolor

History: Believed to have originated in Turkey or Central Asia, there are records of this rose dating back to the fourteenth century. There was once a double form, now thought to be lost.

Description: The name 'Bicolor' comes from the unusual colouring of the petals, which are coppery-orange on the inside and yellow on the reverse. Some branches produce only yellow flowers, having reverted to the original form. It is a spreading shrub rose to 1.5 m (5 ft), with upright stems and masses of flowers at its peak. The foliage is also prolific, bright green and glossy. The flowers have an unusual fragrance which some gardeners find unappealing – hence the species name 'foetida'.

Parentage: Form of *R. foetida*

Other names: 'Austrian Copper', *R. lutea punicea*

Suggested usage: An excellent feature rose for a mixed bed or border, it is also prized for its unusual two-colour flower display.

- ▨ FLOWERS ONCE ONLY
- ▨ TOLERATES SOME SHADE
- ▨ SUSCEPTIBLE TO BLACK SPOT

R. foetida lutea

History: Originally from southwest Asia, this rose naturalized across southern and eastern Europe and was one of the earliest of the cultivated yellow-flowering roses, known in England since before 1600.

Description: A handsome upright shrub rose growing to 3 m (10 ft), it has prickly stems and aromatic, bright green foliage. The single flowers are large and rich golden-yellow, although sometimes they can be seen suffused with red. After flowering the shrub produces brick-red rosehips that are also quite showy. The flowers have quite an unusual fragrance which some gardeners find unappealing.

Parentage: Thought to be a natural hybrid of *R. kokiana* and *R. hemisphaerica*

Other names: 'Austrian Briar', 'Austrian Yellow'

Suggested usage: A useful bushy shrub rose, it is also tolerant of poorer soils, providing it gets plenty of sun. It is great background plant for a mixed flower bed or rose border.

- ▨ FLOWERS ONCE ONLY
- ▨ TOLERATES SOME SHADE
- ▨ SUSCEPTIBLE TO BLACK SPOT

R. foetida persiana

History: An interesting double form of *R. foetida*, introduced to Britain in 1837 from western Asia. Both these ancient roses are responsible for the introduction of yellow flowers into modern rose breeding.

Description: A slightly less vigorous shrub rose than *R. foetida*, this variety grows to 2 m (6½ ft) with masses of small, light green leaves and relatively few thorns on the slender stems. The flowers are double and globular, with rich golden-yellow petals and no perceptible fragrance.

Parentage: Unknown

Other names: 'Persian Yellow'

Suggested usage: This is a shrub rose that is best in hot, dry climates due to its susceptibility to black spot in more humid growing conditions. It makes a wonderful background plant for mixed rose borders or perennial beds. Tolerant of poorer soils and low rainfall, it is a good choice for country gardens.

- FLOWERS ONCE ONLY
- TOLERATES SOME SHADE
- SUSCEPTIBLE TO BLACK SPOT

R. laevigata

History: Originating from China, but later introduced to North America towards the end of the eighteenth century, where it quickly naturalized across the warmer areas.

Description: A vigorous climber that grows to 10 m (33 ft) or more, it tends to hold its foliage right through the winter in warmer regions, to which it is more suited. In colder climates with severe frosts it is frequently lost during winter. The rich dark green foliage is glossy and bright in colour, and the single white flowers are very large and fragrant with outstanding golden-yellow stamens. It is quite a thorny rose, with bristly, pear-shaped red hips in late summer and autumn.

Parentage: Unknown

Other names: Cherokee rose, *R. sinica alba*

Suggested usage: This rose needs a lot of space to really put on a display, clambering over fences or pergolas with rampant ease. It can be cut back severely to control its growth in smaller gardens.

- FLOWERS ONCE ONLY
- TOLERATES SOME SHADE
- DISEASE-RESISTANT

R. x macrantha

History: An old gallica-style rose that was first identified in France in 1880 and was later introduced to Britain.

Description: A vigorous climbing shrub rose, it has lengthy arching stems that can grow to 2 m (6½ ft) or more if left unpruned. The lush green foliage is dark with prominent veining and the single, open flowers are clear pink, fading to white with age. The blooms feature prominent yellow stamens and have a rich fragrance. The hips are globular and a dull red colour, appearing in profusion in autumn. This is an ideal rose for poorer soils or where the garden is shaded for part of the day.

Parentage: *R. gallica* x unknown

Other names: None

Suggested usage: A hardy and fast-growing shrubby climber, it is ideal for training over a trellis or against a sunny wall. Keep it compact with regular pruning of the canes. It is sometimes grown as a groundcover.

- FLOWERS ONCE ONLY
- FULL SUN TO SEMI-SHADE
- DISEASE-RESISTANT

R. moschata

History: First introduced to Britain during the reign of Henry VIII, *R. moschata* is an ancient wild rose. Until recently it was thought to be extinct, but it was rediscovered growing in the wild by an English rosarian.

Description: A climber that grows to 3 m (10 ft), it has sturdy stems with few thorns and soft grey-green foliage. The small, single, creamy white flowers are carried in bountiful clusters, and appear about 4 weeks later in the season than many other wild roses. Once in flower, the rose will continue producing clusters of flowers over 3 months. The flowers have a distinctive musk fragrance that is particularly noticeable when hit by direct sunlight, and are followed in late summer by oval, red hips.

Parentage: Unknown

Other names: Musk rose

Suggested usage: A less vigorous climber, it is a useful rose for smaller gardens where it can be pruned to limit the size. It looks beautiful when grown against a trellis or over a small archway.

- FLOWERS ONCE ONLY
- FULL SUN TO SEMI-SHADE
- DISEASE-RESISTANT

R. moyesii 'Geranium'

One of the best single, red-flowering roses, this charming medium-sized shrub has many fine attributes, including glorious flowers, attractive light green foliage and very showy, orange-red hips in autumn.

The original seedling of *R. moyesii* 'Geranium' was discovered at Wisley Gardens in England in 1938. Growing to 2.5 m (8 ft) in height, it forms an open, upright shrub with rather stiff, arching stems which are clothed in abundant, light green foliage. The stems are made more decorative by the contrasting red thorns – which look good, but can be vicious if care is not taken when pruning. The flowers appear in early summer and are single with rather waxy, crimson-red petals and creamy white stamens.

Many gardeners believe that the elegant, urn-shaped hips of 'Geranium' are even better value than the flowers – the hips are particularly prolific during the autumn months, and are a rich shade of red-orange.

'Geranium' is a hardy and easy to grow rose which has proven to be quite tolerant of poorer soils and is even capable of producing flowers in semi-shaded situations. It doesn't respond well to hard pruning, preferring a light trimming back after flowering and then simply some tidying up of dead wood during the winter months.

■ FLOWERS ONCE ONLY
■ FULL SUN TO SEMI-SHADE
■ DISEASE-RESISTANT

TOP LEFT: 'Geranium' is grown for its abundant and distinctive, long orange hips, as much as for its blooms.
BOTTOM LEFT: 'Geranium' has a compact growing habit, making it ideal for smaller-sized gardens.
OPPOSITE: The blood-red blooms of 'Geranium' are single, with overlapping petals and creamy stamens.

R. pimpinellifolia altaica

History: A charming old rose found growing wild across Europe, from Iceland to France and then across to Turkey. It was introduced into Britain before 1600, where it quickly naturalized.

Description: A delightful small shrub, this rose grows to 1 m (3 ft), and has slender stems densely covered in long, needle-like prickles. The small, single flowers are pink or creamy white and followed by small, purple-black hips in autumn. They have a light fragrance. The foliage is small, bright green and ferny. It suckers freely if allowed, and can be invasive if this characteristic isn't controlled.

Parentage: Unknown

Other names: Burnet rose, *R. spinosissima*, Scotch rose

Suggested usage: A great rose for the front of a mixed border, use it to fill in and around taller-growing species. It is also suitable for a container or as a low, clipped hedge. It tolerates quite sandy, poor soil but likes plenty of summer water.

■ FLOWERS ONCE ONLY
▨ FULL SUN
■ DISEASE-RESISTANT

R. sericea pteracantha

History: A fascinating old rose first introduced to the West from China in 1890. It is a member of the pimpinellifolia family of roses, noted for their small leaves and prickly stems.

Description: This rose is valued more for its bright red, wedge-shaped thorns than for its flowers or foliage – although these are also both worthwhile attributes. It is a shrubby plant growing to 2.5 m (8 ft), with brown stems that feature huge, translucent red thorns that turn grey with age. The flowers are small and white and quite exquisite, and have a light fragrance. The foliage is small, bright green and fern-like.

Parentage: Unknown

Other names: Wing thorn rose

Suggested usage: Plant this rose in full sun so that the light can catch the brilliant thorny stems. It makes a good 'talking point' rose for the collector. Regular pruning encourages new stem growth and thorns.

■ FLOWERS ONCE ONLY
▨ FULL SUN
■ DISEASE-RESISTANT

R. virginiana plena

History: A rose from eastern North America, found growing wild from Pennsylvania to Arkansas. It was introduced to Britain sometime prior to 1870.

Description: An upright, bushy shrub growing to 2 m (6½ ft), it has reddish stems and a good covering of glossy green foliage. The double, clear pink flowers emerge from attractive, pointed buds. The petals scroll as they open, revealing a centre that is a much deeper and richer pink than the edge. The flowers are lightly scented and the foliage tends to russet-coloured in the autumn.

Parentage: Unknown

Other names: 'Rose d'Amour', 'St Mark's Rose'

Suggested usage: Often grown against a wall, this rose is an excellent garden specimen both for its foliage and flowers. It can tolerate quite poor, sandy soil and prefers little or no pruning, except for the removal of dead wood in winter.

- ▣ RECURRENT-FLOWERING
- ▣ FULL SUN TO SEMI-SHADE
- ▣ DISEASE-RESISTANT

R. xanthina 'Canary Bird'

History: An outstanding form of R. xanthina identified in China in 1906, and later found growing wild as far afield as Mongolia and Turkestan.

Description: A graceful, open shrub, it grows to 2 m (6½ ft) in height, and has slender, pendulous stems well covered with prickly thorns. The foliage is very small and rounded, and the clear yellow, single flowers are carried along the stems to create a spectacular display when in full bloom. The flowers have very prominent yellow stamens and produce a rich, sweet scent in summer. In warmer climates it may spot-flower again in autumn.

Parentage: Possibly R. hugonis x R. xanthina

Other names: R. xanthina spontanea

Suggested usage: This is a rather tricky rose to get established unless growing conditions are ideal – rich, moist but well-drained soil and full sun will produce the best results. Prune out dead wood in winter, then lightly shape the shrub as a feature plant.

- ▣ FLOWERS ONCE ONLY
- ▣ FULL SUN
- ▣ DISEASE-RESISTANT

HEIRLOOM
ROSES

The overwhelming popularity of the so-called heirloom, heritage or old-fashioned roses is a reflection of the gardener's love of the soft, sweetly fragrant blooms that characterize these charming old varieties. Many heirloom roses are the result of early attempts at hybridization, while others are accidental crosses that gardeners discovered and found to be excellent garden specimens.

There is a very blurred line between old-fashioned and modern roses, and different books categorize them differently. For some experts the cut-off point is around the 1930s – any rose developed after that point is considered 'modern'. However, these boundaries do shift, and the term 'modern' is therefore more applicable to roses that are strictly classified as hybrid tea roses or floribundas.

Heirloom roses are not just prized for the beauty of their flowers and fragrance. Many are tough and easy to grow in a wide range of soils and climates, and seem to be more disease-resistant than many of their newer counterparts. They require less stringent pruning, and therefore are suited to busy modern gardeners who don't have a lot of time for fussing over their roses.

PREVIOUS PAGE 'Fru Dagmar Hastrup'

'Archduc Joseph'

History: One of the most attractive of the old tea roses, first identified in France in the year 1872.

Description: A large-growing shrub that can reach 1.3 m (4¼ ft) in height, and spreading to 1 m (3 ft), this tea rose has an abundance of deep green, glossy foliage that should clothe the stems and look healthy all through the season. The stems are relatively thornless and the flowers are made up of many petals that are a wonderful mix of pink, purple and orange with golden-yellow overtones. It has the reputation of being quite a tough rose that can survive reasonably harsh growing conditions.

Parentage: Seedling of 'Mme Lombard'

Other names: None

Suggested usage: Its size and growth habit make this rose a suitable hedging shrub or background plant in a border. It has lanky stems which also allow it to be trained as a small climber.

- FLOWERS ONCE ONLY
- FULL SUN
- RELATIVELY DISEASE-FREE

'Belle Isis'

History: A charming old gallica rose developed by the breeder Parmentier in Belgium in the year 1845.

Description: A compact, upright shrub rose, 'Belle Isis' reaches a height of 1.2 m (4 ft), and has a good covering of grey-green foliage that acts as a perfect foil for the flowers. The strongly fragrant blooms are large and fully double with a flat shape and delicate pale pink petals that fade to white as the blooms age. The stems are quite thorny. This rose is one of the parents of the famous 'Constance Spry' rose.

Parentage: Unknown

Other names: None

Suggested usage: 'Belle Isis' is compact enough to be grown in a large pot or tub, or at the front of a mixed rose bed. The stems droop a little, making the mature blooms hard to appreciate.

FLOWERS ONCE ONLY
FULL SUN
RELATIVELY DISEASE-FREE

'Catherine Mermet'

History: An excellent tea rose, developed in France in the year 1869.

Description: A bushy shrub, this rose has a slightly rambling habit that reaches 1.4 m (4½ ft) in height, spreading to 1 m (3 ft). The foliage is mid-green with attractive copper-tinged overtones. The long stems and shapely, pointed flower buds open to semi-double, pale pink to lilac flowers with a creamy yellow base. Because of the long stems it is an excellent rose for cutting.

Parentage: Unknown

Other names: None

Suggested usage: 'Catherine Mermet' is a rose that should be encouraged to develop its own natural shape, with just a little pruning back after flowering.

■ RECURRENT-FLOWERING
▨ FULL SUN
■ RELATIVELY DISEASE-FREE

'Chapeau de Napoléon'

History: An outstanding centifolia rose discovered by chance in 1826 – some experts believe in France and some Switzerland.

Description: The common name 'Chapeau', meaning 'hat', comes from the unusual formation of the calyx, which is said to be in the shape of a cocked hat. This is a particularly beautiful rose, large and fragrant, with cabbage-like, deep silvery-pink flowers that are cup-shaped and fully double. The shrub grows to 1.5 m (5 ft), and has a good bushy shape, although some of the flower stems can be droopy when laden with blooms. The leaves are large and mid-green with a slightly soft and drooping growth habit.

Parentage: Unknown

Other names: 'Crested Moss', 'Cristata'

Suggested usage: This is a centre-stage rose that could easily be a main feature in a bed of old roses. Mass-plant, or plant one rose on its own surrounded by complementary perennials.

■ RECURRENT-FLOWERING
▨ FULL SUN
■ RELATIVELY DISEASE-FREE

'Charles de Mills'

History: A charming gallica rose with an unknown history. The name of the breeder has been lost.

Description: A particularly striking, thornless, shrubby rose, it grows to 1.5 m (5 ft) or more in the right situation, and has lush, deep green foliage that smothers the bush all through the growing season. The flowers are prolific – very large, flat and fully double with petals in a beautiful shade of crimson that fade to a deeper purple or lilac-grey as the blooms age. The flowers are highly fragrant and look wonderful in old-fashioned floral arrangements.

Parentage: Unknown

Other names: 'Bizarre Triomphant'

Suggested usage: This rose can be trained onto a short pillar for a column of massed colour in early summer. Its shrubby shape lends itself well to informal hedging or to hiding an unsightly fence.

■ FLOWERS ONCE ONLY
■ FULL SUN
■ RELATIVELY DISEASE-FREE

R. chinensis 'Viridiflora'

History: This unusual rose is a mutated form of R. chinensis 'Old Blush', and instead of petals it has deformed scales or sepals that create the impression of a green flower. It has been known to rose lovers since 1843.

Description: Growing and spreading to 1 m (3 ft), this rose is grown mainly for its novelty value as the 'flowers' are not really things of beauty, but more a talking point. The foliage is small and mid-green in colour, and the flowers are carried in upright clusters. They open with bracts of bright green that age to rich bronze and russet tonings that look appealing when the entire plant is in full flush. It is very free-flowering, and will reward for many months.

Parentage: Unknown

Other names: Green rose, R. monstrosa, R. viridiflora

Suggested usage: Flower arrangers love this rose because the cut flowers are so unusual. It should be positioned near the front of a garden bed or beside a path where it can be featured and admired.

■ RECURRENT-FLOWERING
■ FULL SUN
■ DISEASE-RESISTANT

'Complicata'

History: A gallica rose with unknown origins, although some experts believe it to be a hybrid with the species *R. canina*.

Description: A handsome, tall shrubby rose, 'Complicata' has arching stems that can reach 3 m (10 ft) in height. It is a fast-growing and vigorous variety with a good covering of small, grey-green foliage and masses of large and very decorative, single flowers that are a clear, bright shade of pink with slightly paler centres and wonderful golden stamens. The flowers can at times measure 12 cm (4¾ inches) across. This rose is valued for its ease of cultivation and tolerance of poorer soils.

Parentage: Unknown

Other names: None

Suggested usage: 'Complicata' has a slightly rambling habit and can be used to scramble into trees or cover ugly fences. It has also been used quite effectively as a pillar or small climbing rose.

- FLOWERS ONCE ONLY
- FULL SUN
- RELATIVELY DISEASE-FREE

'Cornelia'

History: A hybrid musk rose developed by the English breeder Pemberton in 1925.

Description: This vigorous, spreading bush rose can reach 1.5 m (5 ft) in height and branches out even further, with slender dark brown shoots and very showy bronzy foliage that looks lovely even when the plant is not in flower. The blooms are small and carried in large clusters or trusses, each small bloom being a delicate apricot-pink flushed with a deeper pink. When in flower the entire plant exudes a rich, musky fragrance. 'Cornelia' is an excellent cut flower, valued for its lengthy flowering period.

Parentage: Unknown

Other names: None

Suggested usage: This is a stand-out rose bush that should be used as a feature. It combines brilliantly with flowering perennials, or can be mass-planted for a really stunning effect.

- RECURRENT-FLOWERING
- TOLERATES SOME SHADE
- RELATIVELY DISEASE-FREE

'Cottage Maid'

History: A mutated form of *Rosa centifolia* first introduced from France in 1845.

Description: 'Cottage Maid' is an upright, thorny bush to 2 m (6½ ft) in height and spread, with masses of small, mid-green leaves that make it an attractive shrub even when not in flower. The rounded blooms are prolific and a dainty creamy white flushed with pale pink – however they are inclined to be easily damaged by rain. Like all centifolias, this rose is sweetly scented.

Parentage: Unknown

Other names: 'Belles des Jardins', 'La Rubanée'

Suggested usage: A lovely background, shrubby rose for a cottage garden border, it responds well to pruning that will keep growth dense. Beware of the thorns!

▦ FLOWERS ONCE ONLY
▦ FULL SUN
▦ SUSCEPTIBLE TO BLACK SPOT

'Crépuscule'

History: Another early French rose, identified in 1904 and classified as a noisette.

Description: A rambling climber that can reach 3.5 m (11½ ft) in height, this noisette rose has thornless stems and a good covering of deep green foliage that covers the lengthy stems right through the season. The flowers are a delight – semi-double and muddled in appearance, with soft, old-gold to apricot petals. The flowers are fragrant and prolific if the plant is healthy and the spent flowers are routinely deadheaded. Although quite a vigorous climber, it is regarded as somewhat frost-tender in colder climates.

Parentage: Unknown

Other names: None

Suggested usage: This is a delightful climber to encourage into trees and along fencelines, being allowed to develop without much pruning or shaping.

▦ RECURRENT-FLOWERING
▦ FULL SUN
▦ RELATIVELY DISEASE-FREE

'Devoniensis'

History: An outstanding climbing tea rose introduced in England in 1858, developed from the 'Devoniensis' shrub rose, which was an earlier version.

Description: A graceful climbing variety, it can grow to 3.5 m (11½ ft), and has slender, arching stems and a good covering of healthy, light green foliage. The flowers are the most outstanding feature, being very large and creamy yellow in colour, with petals that fold towards the centre. The flowers are also deliciously fragrant, and will keep producing right through the season, even into autumn. This rose does not like extremely cold conditions, and is sometimes grown under glass in the northern hemisphere.

Parentage: Sport of 'Devoniensis'

Other names: 'Magnolia Rose'

Suggested usage: Position this climber against a wall or trellis in a warm and sheltered situation. Deadhead spent flowers routinely to encourage repeat-flowering.

■ RECURRENT-FLOWERING
▨ FULL SUN
■ DISEASE-RESISTANT

'Duchesse de Brabant'

History: A popular old tea rose introduced in France by the breeder Bernede in 1857.

Description: A twiggy shrub, it grows to 1.5 m (5 ft) in height, but tends to spread more widely. The foliage is excellent, prolific and mid-green in colour, and the flowers are very large and cup-shaped with wonderfully translucent, pearly pink petals that really stand out from the background foliage. Its value is in its long flowering time and the abundant flower clusters, hence its popularity with gardeners.

Parentage: Unknown

Other names: 'Comtesse de Labarthe'

Suggested usage: It is often grown as a hedging rose because of its good foliage cover and frequency of flowering. The twiggy, inward-growing stems should be routinely thinned.

■ RECURRENT-FLOWERING
▨ FULL SUN
■ RELATIVELY DISEASE-FREE

'Fantin-Latour'

History: Sometimes classified as a centifolia, sometimes a gallica cross, this rose has unknown origins which is surprising given it was first noted in 1900.

Description: A large and spreading shrub, growing to 2 m (6½ ft), it has dramatic, deep green foliage and smooth, almost thornless stems. The flowers are large and double with soft pink petals that are well scented – more reminiscent of the perfume of alba roses. The flowers are carried in clusters, and start out cup-shaped, opening to a flatter, less formal arrangement. The flower buds are also very decorative.

Parentage: Unknown

Other names: None

Suggested usage: This is a good background, shrubby rose for a mixed flower bed because of its size, and the fact that it doesn't require a lot of pruning – just a trim back after flowering. It can tolerate poorer soils.

■ FLOWERS ONCE ONLY
■ FULL SUN
■ RELATIVELY DISEASE-FREE

'Ferdinand Pichard'

History: One of the most outstanding of the old striped roses, this delightful shrub is classified as a hybrid perpetual and was raised in France in 1921.

Description: A vigorous and shrubby rose, it reaches 2 m (6½ ft) in height, and has a good covering of mid-green foliage. The flowers, which are carried in tight clusters, are cup-shaped with the most wonderfully striped carmine, pink and white petals that fade slightly as the bloom matures. This rose also has a distinctive fragrance, which adds to its immense appeal.

Parentage: Unknown

Other names: None

Suggested usage: This is a rose that should be positioned prominently so that its unusual flowers and strong perfume can be easily appreciated. It is sometimes used for hedging, and is also valued as it will tolerate poorer soils.

■ RECURRENT-FLOWERING
▨ FULL SUN
■ RELATIVELY DISEASE-FREE

'Francis Dubreuil'

History: An old tea rose first identified in France in 1894.

Description: 'Francis Dubreuil' is a gorgeous crimson rose that is not often seen in cultivation. It makes a small, open shrub to 1 m (3 ft) in height, and has very thorny stems and rather sparse foliage which can detract from its overall appearance. The flower buds are slender and pointed, opening to deep crimson blooms that become blowsy and fade slightly as they age. It is worth growing for the flower buds alone.

Parentage: Unknown

Other names: None

Suggested usage: This rose is small enough to be grown in a container, positioned prominently when in flower. Otherwise it makes a pretty addition to a mixed flower bed or border. It will keep flowering if it is regularly deadheaded.

▨ RECURRENT-FLOWERING
▨ FULL SUN
▨ RELATIVELY DISEASE-FREE

R. gallica officinalis

History: The oldest known cultivated form of *R. gallica*, this rose was taken from Damascus to France in the thirteenth century. Its aromatic properties were much admired by apothecaries, hence its common name.

Description: A shrub with a spreading, suckering habit, it grows to 1.5 m (5 ft) and has coarse, greyish green foliage that makes a perfect backdrop for the flowers. Blooming slightly later in the season than most gallicas, the entire shrub should be smothered with large, semi-double flowers that are a light crimson with prominent yellow stamens. The scent of this rose is outstanding, as are the small hips that appear in late summer.

Parentage: Ancient form of *R. gallica*

Other names: 'Apothecary's Rose', 'Red Rose of Lancaster', *R. gallica* 'Maxima'

Suggested usage: Feature this rose prominently in the landscape because of its strong perfume and free-flowering habit. It makes a wonderful clipped hedge in a more formal garden, and it tolerates poorer soils.

▨ FLOWERS ONCE ONLY
▨ FULL SUN
▨ DISEASE-RESISTANT

'General Gallieni'

History: An unusual old tea rose, bred in France in 1899, it became one of the most popular roses of its day.

Description: A fast-growing, vigorous shrub rose, reaching 1.2 m (4 ft) in height, 'General Gallieni' is sometimes grown as a standard. The stems have few thorns and a dense covering of glossy, mid-green foliage. The flowers are the main attraction, having a slightly squarish look because of the way the petals are folded. The colours vary from red and pink smudged with cream to buff yellow and deep red according to the summer climate. It is lightly tea-scented.

Parentage: 'Souvenir de Thérèse Levet' x 'Reine Emma des Pays-Bas'

Other names: None

Suggested usage: Allow plenty of space for this rose to grow and spread, or prune it hard to keep the long stem growth under control. The unusual flowers make a good talking point.

■ RECURRENT-FLOWERING
▨ FULL SUN
■ RELATIVELY DISEASE-FREE

RECURRENT-FLOWERING
FULL SUN
SUSCEPTIBLE TO BLACK SPOT

'Gloire de Dijon'

History: A popular old climbing variety, bred in France in 1853 by crossing a yellow tea rose with a creamy pink bourbon rose.

Description: This vigorous climbing rose can grow to 3.5 m (11½ ft) in the right conditions, and has deep green foliage that is sadly prone to black spot in the summer. However, the flowers are spectacular – large, flat and quartered with soft creamy apricot petals that are sometimes tinged with orange. The flowers fall apart if it rains, and therefore a climate with a hot, dry summer is preferable.

Parentage: Unknown tea rose x 'Souvenir de la Malmaison'

Other names: 'Old Glory Rose'

Suggested usage: This is a tremendous climber for growing on archways, trellis or against walls. It can be allowed to climb into trees or cover unsightly fences.

R. hippolyte

History: Known and prized in cultivation since the early nineteenth century.

Description: Considered to be one of the best gallicas, this attractive bushy shrub grows to 1.2 m (4 ft), and has virtually thornless stems covered in smooth, deep green foliage that remains healthy right through the season. The outstanding magenta-purple flowers are carried in clusters which tend to hang down when in full bloom, but are still wonderful for cutting. Each bloom is perfectly formed with paler highlights towards the button-like centre.

Parentage: Of gallica origin, unknown parentage

Other names: 'Souvenir de Kean'

Suggested usage: The shrub is small enough to be grown as a feature rose in a container, positioned prominently when in flower. Pruning it each season by one third will improve form and flowering, and keep it compact.

'Honorine de Brabant'

History: A charming old bourbon rose whose origins and parentage are not known by rosarians.

Description: This is a delightful rose with striped petals that is popular with lovers of heirloom varieties. It grows into a rather open shrub about 1.5 m (5 ft) in height, with masses of lush foliage carried on slender, almost thornless stems. The flowers are prolific, with petals of pale pink, with lilac to purple stripes and sometimes a splattering of the darker shades in between. Each flower is quite large and showy, although sometimes the blooms can be overwhelmed by the foliage.

Parentage: Unknown

Other names: None

Suggested usage: The longer slender stems can be trained onto a low trellis, forming a mini climber. It can also be pruned into a compact shrub by removing old twiggy growth and dead wood.

- RECURRENT-FLOWERING
- TOLERATES SOME SHADE
- RELATIVELY DISEASE-FREE

'Jacques Cartier'

History: A hybrid between a Portland rose and an old China variety, bred in France in 1868.

Description: A compact but upright-growing shrub to 1.2 m (4 ft), it has excellent mid-green foliage and a naturally attractive shape. The showy flowers are very large and fully double with a wonderful old-fashioned shape and clear pink petals that fade to a paler shade of pink around the edges. The flowers are sweetly fragrant and very good for cutting.

Parentage: Unknown

Other names: None

Suggested usage: An adaptable shrub for mixed flower beds and rose borders, it can be positioned towards the centre because of its size and shape. It will reward with a lengthy flowering period.

- RECURRENT-FLOWERING
- FULL SUN
- RELATIVELY DISEASE-FREE

'Königin von Dänemark'

History: This wonderful old rose was bred in Denmark in 1826, and is believed to be a cross between a damask and an alba rose.

Description: An outstanding open shrub rose, it grows to to 1.5 m (5 ft), and has slender, thorny stems that at times are weighed down with blooms. The foliage is rather coarse and blue-green in colour, while the flowers are small and bright pink with an unusual button-eye centre that is most attractive. The colour of the flowers fades as they mature; however, the strong perfume holds for the entire flowering period.

Parentage: Unknown

Other names: 'Belle Courtisane', 'Queen of Denmark'

Suggested usage: Traditionally used as a hedging rose, it responds well to pruning to encourage a denser shape. A very good addition to any old rose garden.

- ▉ FLOWERS ONCE ONLY
- ▉ TOLERATES SOME SHADE
- ▉ RELATIVELY DISEASE-FREE

'Lady Hillingdon'

History: An old-fashioned tea rose developed by English breeders Lowe and Shawer in 1910.

Description: This consistently popular tea rose has gloriously perfumed yellow flowers and glossy, purple-green foliage. It grows to a height of 80 cm (2½ ft) and will spread to 60 cm (2 ft) in width after 2 or more years' growth. It produces plum-coloured new shoots covered in deeply purple-green foliage and the flower buds are long and slender in a rich shade of yellow. They open to loosely filled, double blooms that fade to a much softer shade of yellow. The flowers appear almost continuously from spring to late autumn. The plant has very few thorns and the flowers are good for picking.

Parentage: 'Papa Gontier' x 'Mme Hoste'

Other names: None

Suggested usage: It can be mass-planted for a brilliant display of flowers, and is perfect for a mixed flower bed, underplanted with perennials.

- ▉ RECURRENT-FLOWERING
- ▉ FULL SUN
- ▉ CAN BE CONTAINER-GROWN
- ▉ DISEASE-RESISTANT

'La Reine Victoria'

History: An attractive bourbon rose with rounded blooms, raised in France in 1872.

Description: A charming old rose, this is a slender, upright shrub that grows to 1.2 m (4 ft) in height, with long, slender stems that produce along their entire length, creating a most outstanding display. The foliage is a soft green and creates a pretty backdrop to the cup-shaped flowers which are a rich lilac-pink colour with a silky texture. It can grow very long and leggy if left unpruned.

Parentage: Unknown

Other names: 'Reine Victoria', 'The Shell Rose'

Suggested usage: A feature plant because of the beauty of the flowering stems, it is quite a demanding rose that must have good soil and a hot, dry summer to produce good results.

- RECURRENT-FLOWERING
- FULL SUN
- SUSCEPTIBLE TO BLACK SPOT

'Lorraine Lee'

History: The most famous of the Australian-bred roses, classified as a tea rose and bred in 1924.

Description: A descendant of the wild *Rosa gigantea*, this large-growing and vigorous rose bush can reach 3 m (10 ft) or more in the right situation, and has lush green foliage that is both glossy and healthy. The flowers are elegant and semi-double, with petals that are a blend of rosy pink and apricot. It has a rich fruity fragrance and the overall effect is an absolute delight.

Parentage: 'Jessie Clarke' x 'Capitaine Miller'

Other names: None

Suggested usage: Make a feature of this rose, which can either be allowed to grow to its full size and be a rampant bush, or be pruned back hard as a tidy garden shrub.

■ RECURRENT-FLOWERING
▨ FULL SUN
■ RELATIVELY DISEASE-FREE

■ RECURRENT-FLOWERING
■ TOLERATES SOME SHADE
■ RELATIVELY DISEASE-FREE

'Mme Alfred Carrière'

History: Bred in France in 1879, this noisette rose has long been popular with gardeners.

Description: A very worthwhile white rose, it grows to 5 m (16½ ft) in height, and is therefore usually allowed to grow as a climber. The upward growth is vigorous each season and the stems are blessed with very few thorns but an abundance of light green, healthy foliage. The double flowers are loose and open, cup-shaped and milky white with occasional smudges of pink, and have a wonderful heady fragrance.

Parentage: Unknown

Other names: None

Suggested usage: This rose needs plenty of space to clamber and display its true form. It can be allowed to climb into trees and is ideal for growing over archways due to its lack of thorns. It can be pruned back vigorously to control its size in smaller gardens.

■ RECURRENT-FLOWERING
▨ FULL SUN
■ RELATIVELY DISEASE-FREE

'Parson's Pink China'

History: A rose with a long history in cultivation, it is considered to be one of the first of the old China roses, introduced to Sweden from China in 1752.

Description: 'Parson's Pink China' can be maintained as a small shrub, growing only to 60 cm (2 ft), or allowed upright growth as a compact climber. It has virtually thornless stems and healthy, mid-green foliage. The silvery pink blooms are soft and charming, and continue to flower almost continuously through the season, making it a prized addition to an heirloom rose garden. The flowers have a strong fragrance similar to sweet peas and can be used as cut flowers even though the stems are quite fragile.

Parentage: Unknown

Other names: 'Monthly Rose', 'Old Blush', 'Pallida'

Suggested usage: Make a feature of this rose for its perfume and for its lengthy flowering period. It is sometimes grown as a low hedging plant, being lightly pruned to maintain the shape.

'Pompom de Bourgogne'

History: A very old, dwarf centifolia rose that has been known in cultivation since 1664, although its actual origins are unknown.

Description: Growing to less than 1 m (3 ft) in height, this compact-growing shrub is rather dense and twiggy with a good covering of small green leaves. The growth is mainly upright, with lots of inward-growing stems that should be pruned out to give the shrub a more open shape. The flowers are small and charming, and a rich shade of claret or purple, often flecked with pale pink. They are rounded and make a very pretty display as they cover the entire bush in early summer.

Parentage: Unknown

Other names: *R. burgundica, R. centifolia* 'Parvifolia'

Suggested usage: One of the best old miniature roses, it is ideal for growing in a pot or tub on a balcony or patio where it can enjoy full sun. It is also useful as a low hedging rose along the front of a mixed flower border.

▨ FLOWERS ONCE ONLY
▧ FULL SUN
▪ RELATIVELY DISEASE-FREE

Rugosa roses

The charming rugosa roses are not only attractive, with their lush, dark green foliage and large, papery blooms, but they are also highly valued by gardeners for their resistance to fungal diseases such as black spot.

Rugosa roses are highly varied. However the majority of the blooms are large and single, with fine, papery petals and prominent yellow stamens. Rosy pink, pale pink and white are the most common colours, however there are also yellow and double-flowering forms that are very attractive.

Rugosas make great hedging plants, and should be positioned away from paths because of their rough stems and often sharp thorns.

- ◼ RECURRENT FLOWERING
- ◼ TOLERATES SOME SHADE
- ◼ RELATIVELY DISEASE-FREE

This extensive group of easy-to-grow old roses originated in China, Korea and Japan from where they were taken to Western gardens in the late 1700s. At that time rugosa roses didn't prove to be as popular as many of the other imported wild varieties, probably because of their rather rough, leathery leaves and the fact that most species flower only once in the season.

However for gardeners in difficult and humid climates, rugosa roses are probably the most easy-care of all the old rose varieties, as most resist black spot and other common fungal diseases. Their flowering is often spasmodic, with spot flowers appearing from late spring into autumn rather than one massive show. Most varieties are also prized for their outstanding hips – a feature that makes them appealing in the garden when other roses have well and truly finished for the season.

Favourite rugosa roses

'Fru Dagmar Hastrup': Single, cup-shaped, cinnamon-scented, pale pink blooms.
R. rugosa: Single, cup-shaped, scented, carmine-red blooms.
R. rugosa alba: White blooms.
R. rugosa rosea: Rose-pink blooms.
R. rugosa rubra: Purplish red blooms.
R. rugosa scabrosa: Single, cup-shaped, scented, reddish mauve blooms.
'Roseraie de l'Haÿ: Flat to cup-shaped, double, strongly scented, purplish red blooms.

ABOVE LEFT *Rosa rugosa alba*
OPPOSITE *Rosa rugosa scabrosa*

'Rosa Mundi'

History: Cultivated since the sixteenth century, this variegated form of the gallica rose is considered the oldest and best of the striped roses.

Description: A virtually thornless shrub, it grows to 1.2 m (4 ft), with a dense covering of matt green foliage that provides a perfect foil for the showy flowers. The flowers are striped in shades of light red, pink and white with petals that open out softly from the large clusters of yellow stamens in the centre. It has a gentle fragrance and makes an excellent cut flower.

Parentage: Either a hybrid of *R. gallica* x *R. pendulina* or a sport of *R. gallica*.

Other names: *R. gallica* 'Variegata', *R. gallica* 'Versicolor'

Suggested usage: Another rose that should be used as a feature, prune it in late winter to prevent the flowering stems from being too long and flopping when the flowers appear. It could be used as a hedge at the front of a rose bed. It will grow even in poorer soils.

▨ RECURRENT-FLOWERING
▨ FULL SUN
▨ RELATIVELY DISEASE-FREE

'Souvenir de la Malmaison'

History: Considered to be the most beautiful of the bourbon roses, it was bred in France in 1843.

Description: An outstanding shrub rose growing to 1.2 m (4 ft), it has slender stems covered with a mass of mid-green foliage that looks fantastic when young and healthy, but is prone to fungal problems in wet weather. The flowers are also sensitive to these conditions, and will 'ball' after rainfall. Each bloom is large, double and quartered, with delicate pale pink petals and a fragrance that is said to be a blend of cinnamon and ripe bananas. It is only suitable for hot, dry summers.

Parentage: 'Mme Desprez' x unknown tea rose

Other names: 'Fragrance', 'Queen of Beauty'

Suggested usage: In the right climate this rose makes a wonderful feature plant, positioned prominently in a border or as a specimen on its own. It responds well to extra fertilizing that will encourage even more flowers.

▨ RECURRENT-FLOWERING
▨ FULL SUN
▨ SUSCEPTIBLE TO BLACK SPOT

'Stanwell Perpetual'

History: A delightful Scottish rose that was the result of an accidental cross between a pimpinellifolia and a damask rose in Britain in 1838.

Description: As the name implies, this handsome rose flowers virtually right through the season, from late spring into autumn. It forms a dense and leafy shrub growing to about 1.5 m (5 ft) in height, and has small, grey-green foliage that sometimes colours to russet in autumn. The dainty, sweetly scented flowers are blush-pink, fading to white as they age. This is considered to be one of the best pimpinellifolias.

Parentage: *R. damascena* x *R. pimpinellifolia*

Other names: None

Suggested usage: This is often grown in the northern hemisphere as a hedging rose because of its long flowering period. If used as such it will need shaping during winter to maintain the effect.

▨ RECURRENT-FLOWERING
▨ FULL SUN
▨ RELATIVELY DISEASE-FREE

'Variegata de Bologna'

History: An unusual bourbon rose raised in Italy in 1909, popular with those who love variegated or striped flowers.

Description: A vigorous, arching shrub, it reaches 1.8 m (6 ft) in height, and has strong, thorny stems that have only a light covering of coarse, mid-green foliage. The flowers, however, are quite spectacular. Each bloom is large and cup-shaped with double petals that are creamy white and patterned with stripes and splashes of a rich crimson-purple. The flowers are also highly fragrant which adds greatly to their charm.

Parentage: Unknown

Other names: None

Suggested usage: A stand-out rose for prominent display, it makes a wonderful central rose in a mixed flower border, where the canes can be cut back by one third to encourage denser, bushier growth.

▨ RECURRENT-FLOWERING
▨ FULL SUN
▨ RELATIVELY DISEASE-FREE

ENGLISH
ROSES

David Austin is a legendary English rose breeder who has been developing a unique range of roses for more than 30 years. Using all the techniques developed by modern breeders, he has introduced a range of roses that feature the most appealing characteristics of old roses, yet with some of the recurrent-flowering benefits of the more modern varieties such as hybrid tea roses. His collection is generically known as 'English roses'.

Most David Austin rose blooms are large and soft, with an open flower that is reminiscent of some of the old gallica, damask or centifolia roses. Indeed he has often used these old varieties as the parents of his modern offspring. However, he has also attempted to develop stronger stems that will carry the large, full-blown blooms more efficiently. The end result is roses that are fantastic for picking for indoor display, including many that still carry the strong perfume of their forebears. There are also many beautiful 'single' English roses in his range, which – unlike the wild roses from which they were bred – will flower recurrently right through the season.

These roses, however, do require attention from the gardener. They seem to be quite heavy feeders and the stems can become sparse after several years' growth – some nurseries recommend planting two or more of the same variety in a clump to maintain a bushy effect. Routine pruning through the growing season also helps to maintain bushy, luxuriant growth. Many are also prone to black spot disease and therefore may require routine spraying in more humid climates.

PREVIOUS PAGE 'Troilus'

'Canterbury'

History: A charming old-world variety developed by Austin in 1969.

Description: A small-growing shrub, it rarely reaches more than 40 cm (1¼ ft) in height, with slender stems and a good covering of matt, mid-green foliage. The blooms are huge and almost simple in their petal formation, in a warm pink that fades to almost white as they age. Like many Austin roses, this gem has showy yellow stamens in the centre and also enjoys a delicate fragrance. The small size of the bush compared with the large size of the flowers is most unusual.

Parentage: 'Monique' x 'Constance Spry'

Other names: None

Suggested usage: 'Canterbury' is a perfect rose for a container due to its compact size and showy blooms. Keep trimming away the spent flowers and feeding this rose right through summer and you will enjoy an almost continuous display of flowers.

- RECURRENT-FLOWERING
- FULL SUN
- CAN BE CONTAINER-GROWN
- RELATIVELY DISEASE-FREE

'Charles Austin'

History: One of Austin's most famous and popular varieties, bred in 1973.

Description: A vigorous and upright-growing shrub, this rose reaches 1.5 m (5 ft) or more in height at maturity. It has strong stems and a lush covering of leathery, mid-green foliage which works as a perfect backdrop for the showy flowers. Each flower is very large and cup-shaped, with a multitude of petals in a rich shade of creamy yellow with overtones of warm apricot. The flowers are carried in clusters on stems that are sturdy enough to carry their weight. The fragrance of the flowers is rich and fruity. This is an outstanding variety.

Parentage: 'Chaucer' x 'Aloha'

Other names: None

Suggested usage: Plant a row of 'Charles Austin' roses to create a flower-filled hedge around a rose border. Or use it as the centrepiece of a perennial bed planted in warmer tones of yellow, apricot and orange with just a splash of red.

■ RECURRENT-FLOWERING
■ FULL SUN
■ RELATIVELY DISEASE-FREE

'Emanuel'

History: A wonderful variety that was first bred in 1986, using the popular 'Iceberg' rose for some of its strong characteristics.

Description: A bushy and shapely shrub, this grows to 1.2 m (4 ft) in height and spreads to 1 m (3 ft) as it matures. The foliage is mid-green and should continuously cover the plant through spring and summer. The old-fashioned style flowers are large, double and quartered, with delicate pink petals with a lemon base. The blooms are prized for their sweet, strong perfume.

Parentage: ('Chaucer' x 'Parade') x (seedling x 'Iceberg')

Other names: 'Ausel', 'Emmanuelle'

Suggested usage: A good, low hedging rose, it is also suitable for a large container that can be placed in a prominent position when in full bloom. It needs lots of fertilizer to perform well, and should be routinely deadheaded to encourage recurrent flowering.

▓ RECURRENT-FLOWERING
▓ FULL SUN
▓ CAN BE CONTAINER-GROWN
▓ SUSCEPTIBLE TO BLACK SPOT

'English Garden'

History: A popular shrub rose from the David Austin collection, developed in 1986.

Description: A small but upright-growing shrub, it reaches 1 m (3 ft) in height at maturity. It forms a rounded bush of healthy, deep green foliage and from late spring until autumn it should be topped by a wonderful display of showy blooms. Each flower is bowl-shaped with dense, overlapping petals that are a wonderful shade of golden-cream, appearing more yellow towards the centre. The flowers are also richly perfumed, which adds to the overall appeal.

Parentage: ('Lilian Austin' x seedling) x 'Iceberg'

Other names: 'Ausbuf'

Suggested usage: 'English Garden' is a tough and hardy rose bush that can be used as a feature in a mixed flower border or mass-planted for a fantastic effect in summer. Routine feeding and deadheading of spent blooms is essential to maintain a good display.

▓ RECURRENT-FLOWERING
▓ FULL SUN
▓ CAN BE CONTAINER-GROWN
▓ RELATIVELY DISEASE-FREE

'Fisherman's Friend'

History: A less commonly grown English rose, developed in 1987.

Description: A vigorous and fast-growing shrubby rose, this should reach 1.2 m (4 ft) or more in height at maturity. The sturdy stems are clothed in rich, mid-green foliage that should remain healthy all through the season if overhead watering is avoided. The flowers are very large and full in the old-fashioned style, with petals in a rich shade of crimson. 'Fisherman's Friend' is not known for its fragrance; however, the blooms are excellent for cutting, due to their strong, upright stems.

Parentage: Unknown

Other names: 'Auschild'

Suggested usage: A pretty rose for an old-fashioned flower border, it responds well to routine cutting back and deadheading and will benefit from some extra fertilizer during the growing season.

▨ RECURRENT-FLOWERING
▨ FULL SUN
▨ CAN BE CONTAINER-GROWN
▨ RELATIVELY DISEASE-FREE

'Golden Celebration'

History: One of the largest-flowering of the English roses, bred by Austin in 1987.

Description: A shapely rounded shrub, this grows to 1.2 m (4 ft) and has arching stems of relatively disease-free, mid-green foliage. The flowers are huge with rich golden-yellow petals that fade to a soft yellow as they age. The flowers are quite rounded, creating a showy display as they emerge one after another in small but dense clusters. The flower buds are also particularly attractive. The strong fragrance is reminiscent of old tea roses, with a slight sweet strawberry overtone.

Parentage: Unknown

Other names: 'Ausgold'

Suggested usage: This vigorous rose is tall enough to train on a trellis as a short climber, or it can be maintained as a shrub if routinely shaped from the beginning of the season.

▨ RECURRENT-FLOWERING
▨ FULL SUN
▨ RELATIVELY DISEASE-FREE

'Graham Thomas'

History: Considered by David Austin to be one of his finest roses, bred in 1983, and named after another enthusiastic rose breeder.

Description: A vigorous and bushy shrub rose, 'Graham Thomas' grows to 1.2 m (4 ft) in height and spreads to I m (3 ft). The foliage is lush and mid-green in colour and, in summer, the entire shrub is covered with a massive display of very large, softly cup-shaped blooms which are a deep, pure yellow with hints of apricot during their early stages of opening. The flowers are strongly tea-scented and a prized cut bloom, growing in large clusters over many months.

Parentage: 'Charles Austin' x ('Iceberg' x seedling)

Other names: 'Ausmas'

Suggested usage: This is a rose to feature in a mixed bed or border, or to mass-plant along a fenceline as a flowering hedge. Routine picking of the flowers encourages new growth and even more flowers as the season continues.

■ RECURRENT-FLOWERING
■ FULL SUN
■ SUSCEPTIBLE TO BLACK SPOT

'Heritage'

History: A modern shrub rose bred by Austin in 1984.

Description: A fast-growing, vigorous bush, 'Heritage' reaches 1.2 m (4 ft) in height, and has small, deep green leaves that are slightly glossy. The flowers are large and showy and cup-shaped with pale, shell-pink petals. The blooms have a rich, lemony fragrance and are excellent for cut flowers.

Parentage: Seedling x 'Iceberg' seedling

Other names: 'Ausblush'

Suggested usage: This is a rose that responds well to rich soils and good growing conditions. It can be blended with other pastel pink and apricot flowers, or grown in a container to great effect.

▓ RECURRENT-FLOWERING
▓ FULL SUN
▓ CAN BE CONTAINER-GROWN
▓ RELATIVELY DISEASE-FREE

'L. D. Braithwaite'

History: A charming old-fashioned David Austin rose bred in the 1970s.

Description: This is a vigorous, upright shrub, growing to 1.2 m (4 ft) with fairly sturdy stems, and a good covering of mid-green foliage during the flowering season. The flowers are considered to have the brightest crimson colouring of any of David Austin's varieties – each bloom is large and slightly cup-shaped, and opens out widely as it matures. The flowers are prolific and are carried in small clusters that make wonderful indoor displays – especially if each of the blooms is at a different stage of opening.

Parentage: 'Mary Rose' x seedling

Other names: 'Auscrim'

Suggested usage: The extreme brilliance of this flower colour makes this rose very special – it can be used as a dramatic contrast in a bed of blue or purple-flowering perennials or mass-planted.

▓ RECURRENT-FLOWERING
▓ TOLERATES SOME SHADE
▓ CAN BE CONTAINER-GROWN
▓ RELATIVELY DISEASE-FREE

'Leander'

History: An adaptable old-style rose variety bred by Austin in 1982.

Description: One of the largest-growing Austin varieties, it reaches 2 m (6½ ft) or more in height when grown in a good situation. The lush, healthy foliage that clothes the long, arching stems is mid-green in colour and slightly glossy. The flowers are small and fully double, in a rich shade of creamy pink. They are carried in clusters and have the added charm of a sweet, heady perfume.

Parentage: 'Charles Austin' x seedling

Other names: 'Auslea'

Suggested usage: This vigorous rose can be grown and trained as a climber to cover a trellis or archway. Alternatively, it can be kept pruned back through the season to produce a more bushy, compact shrub.

- RECURRENT-FLOWERING
- FULL SUN
- DISEASE-RESISTANT

'Lilian Austin'

History: An outstanding rose bred in 1973, it has been popular ever since.

Description: A shapely, rounded shrub, it grows to 1.2 m (4 ft) in height, and has quite lush and healthy mid-green foliage that makes an excellent foil for the flowers. From late spring onwards it produces prolific blooms on its curved, arching stems. The flowers are cup-shaped and double with petals in a strong shade of pink with slightly wavy edges, giving each bloom a frilled appearance.

Parentage: 'Aloha' x 'The Yeoman'

Other names: None

Suggested usage: 'Lilian Austin' makes quite a handsome rose for a flower border, or as a specimen in a bed of lower-growing annuals. It responds well to watering at ground level and additional mulch in summer.

■ RECURRENT-FLOWERING
■ FULL SUN
■ DISEASE-RESISTANT

'Mary Rose'

History: A perennial favourite in the Austin collection, bred in 1983, and named to honour the recovery of Henry VIII's flagship from the Solent River in Britain.

Description: A good-shaped, rounded shrub, this reaches 1.2 m (4 ft) in height if well fertilized and protected from diseases. The stems are upright with mid-green, matt foliage and the flowers are very large, cup-shaped and double, in a strong shade of clear pink that darkens slightly with age. The flowers are also slightly perfumed.

Parentage: Seedling x 'The Friar'

Other names: 'Ausmary'

Suggested usage: A pretty pink rose for a pastel flower border, it can also be pruned to keep it compact and grown in a container. It looks wonderful when underplanted with white-flowering annuals.

■ RECURRENT-FLOWERING
■ FULL SUN
■ DISEASE-RESISTANT
■ CAN BE CONTAINER-GROWN

'Prospero'

History: Prized for the fragrance of the flowers, this variety was bred by Austin in 1982.

Description: A small, shrubby rose, 'Prospero' never seems to develop a good shape and lacks outstanding foliage. However, the flowers are absolutely beautiful, in a strong shade of wine-red that matures to a deep grape-purple, covering the entire plant in early summer. The blooms are also richly fragrant, making them excellent cut flowers to bring indoors.

Parentage: 'The Knight' x seedling

Other names: 'Auspero'

Suggested usage: To disguise the somewhat uninspiring overall shape of this rose, underplantings of perennials are desirable. Routine picking of the flowers will help a little. Alternatively, the rose can be grown in a cutting garden where overall appearance is not so important.

■ RECURRENT-FLOWERING
■ FULL SUN
■ SUSCEPTIBLE TO BLACK SPOT

'Redouté'

History: Named in honour of the famous French botanical artist, and bred in Britain in the 1980s by Austin, it was a sport of 'Mary Rose'.

Description: This is a charming, old-fashioned style rose, with slightly paler and more translucent petals than its parent. Growing to 1.2 m (4 ft) in height, with an overall good shape and covering of foliage, it produces very large, cup-shaped flowers that are fully double in a delicate shade of pink. Its fragrance is subtle and fruity and it should reward with constant flowering if well maintained.

Parentage: Sport of 'Mary Rose'

Other names: 'Auspale'

Suggested usage: 'Redouté' is a lovely, soft pink rose ideal for a dainty border of pastels, or as a contrast to blue- or purple-flowering perennials. It can be kept trimmed and grown in a large container – two or more grown together will produce a fuller effect.

- RECURRENT-FLOWERING
- FULL SUN
- CAN BE CONTAINER-GROWN
- RELATIVELY DISEASE-FREE

'Sharifa Asma'

History: One of the prettiest of the pale pink English roses, bred in the 1980s.

Description: A well-formed, rounded shrub, this rose grows to 1.2 m (4 ft) with fairly plentiful, mid-green foliage that, if healthy, makes a perfect backdrop for the outstanding flowers. Each bloom is very large and showy, producing rosettes of petals in a delicate shade of blush-pink. The flowers are prolific if the shrub is well grown, and they are also sweetly fragrant, with a hint of grape and mulberry.

Parentage: 'Mary Rose' x 'Admired Miranda'

Other names: 'Ausreef'

Suggested usage: A useful rose because of its good shape and excellent flowers, it prefers a semi-shaded situation because harsh summer sun can easily damage the delicate pale petals. Routine picking of the flowers improves overall blooming.

- RECURRENT-FLOWERING
- TOLERATES SOME SHADE
- CAN BE CONTAINER-GROWN
- SUSCEPTIBLE TO BLACK SPOT

'Shropshire Lass'

History: An older Austin variety, but one that he continues to recommend highly to rose growers.

Description: This is quite a vigorous, large-growing shrub that can reach 1.8 m (6 ft). It produces sturdy stems clothed in masses of mid-green, slightly glossy foliage. The flower buds are a dainty apricot-pink colour, opening to the palest pink flowers with prominent and showy yellow stamens. The blooms have a strong, sweet fragrance that remains in the air all through the flowering period. This variety has tremendous old-fashioned appeal.

Parentage: Unknown

Other names: None

Suggested usage: The vigorous and arching growth habit of this rose makes it suited to training as a climber against a wall trellis. It can also be trimmed routinely to keep it compact as a shrub.

- FLOWERS ONCE ONLY
- FULL SUN
- SUSCEPTIBLE TO BLACK SPOT

'The Prince'

History: Carrying some of the characteristics of the old gallicas, this gem was bred by Austin in the 1980s.

Description: A small and compact shrub that grows to 60 cm (2 ft), with moderately lush, medium to dark green foliage, this rose is grown mainly for its showy flowers. The blooms are in the purple, lavender and lilac colour range, making it an unusual feature. Each bloom is large and fully double with a quartered appearance and masses of petals that emerge as crimson but quickly turn to a shade of rich purple. The flowers have a rich, old-rose fragrance, that greatly adds to their charm.

Parentage: Unknown

Other names: 'Ausvelvet'

Suggested usage: A rose for container cultivation, it can be kept compact and shrubby with routine pruning and will flower right through the season if deadheaded regularly. Combine it with other purple- and lilac-flowering annuals and perennials.

- RECURRENT-FLOWERING
- FULL SUN
- CAN BE CONTAINER-GROWN
- SUSCEPTIBLE TO BLACK SPOT

'Troilus'

History: A worthwhile rose in the apricot colour range, bred by David Austin in 1983.

Description: A strong-growing and well-formed rose shrub that can reach 1.3 m (4½ ft) in height when grown in a good situation. The sturdy stems are covered with mid-green, matt foliage that works well as a foil for the large, showy blooms. Each flower is deeply cup-shaped with masses of petals that are a wonderful shade of creamy apricot. The flowers are also highly fragrant, with sweet honey overtones. The flowers are considered excellent for cutting.

Parentage: Seedling cross

Other names: None

Suggested usage: A stand-out rose to use as a special feature in the garden, it can be used to frame a garden bed or grown against a wall for a sunny summer display. Regular cutting of the flowers encourages further growth.

- RECURRENT-FLOWERING
- FULL SUN
- CAN BE CONTAINER-GROWN
- RELATIVELY DISEASE-FREE

'Wildflower'

History: A delightful small-growing rose bred by Austin in 1986, with characteristics of wild field roses, hence the common name.

Description: 'Wildflower' is a cottage-style garden rose prized for its continuous flowering and low growing habit. It forms a spreading shrub no more than 45 cm (1½ ft) in height, and has masses of twiggy stem growth and small, mid-green leaves. The flowers are very simple in form, and single, with pale apricot-pink petals and golden-yellow stamens.

Parentage: 'Lilian Austin' x ('Canterbury' x 'Golden Wings')

Other names: None

Suggested usage: Most commonly grown as a groundcover, this rose makes a wonderful understorey planting for other roses in a similar colour range. Or use it as the edging of a mixed flower or perennial border. It also makes a pretty potted specimen.

- RECURRENT-FLOWERING
- FULL SUN
- CAN BE CONTAINER-GROWN
- SUSCEPTIBLE TO BLACK SPOT

HYBRID TEA
ROSES

Also classified by rosarians as large-flowered bush roses, these modern wonders owe their good looks and charm to the best features of the hybrid perpetual and old tea roses, from which they were originally bred. The aim was to capture the beauty of those high-pointed buds that made the old tea roses so sought after, and also to develop some of the recurrent-flowering characteristics of the hybrid perpetuals. Long, strong stems are also a dominant feature of hybrid tea roses, developed so that the flowers can be used for picking – never flopping over with the weight of the bloom, like so many of the old-fashioned varieties.

Hybrid tea roses have been in development for nearly 100 years, and during this time literally thousands of new roses have been introduced to keen gardeners. Many of them fall by the wayside as new and so-called 'better' varieties are introduced, and just a few remain popular right through the decades, because of their outstanding flowering and ease of cultivation.

PREVIOUS PAGE 'Double Delight'

'Alexander'

History: Bred by the Harkness family in Britain in 1972.

Description: This is a rose that produces an outstanding, upright, bushy shrub to 1.5 m (5 ft) in height, and has masses of deep green, glossy foliage that is extremely resistant to fungal problems. The flowers are very large and carried in clusters, opening from pointed buds to produce bright vermilion-red flowers that are perfect for cutting. As the blooms open the petals seem more loosely arranged, giving a softer appearance. The flowers have a light, sweet fragrance.

Parentage: 'Super Star' x ('Ann Elizabeth' x 'Allgold')

Other names: 'Alexandra'

Suggested usage: 'Alexander' is a very versatile rose that can be used as a specimen or a tall hedging rose to hide an unattractive fenceline. Regular cutting and a good pruning in late summer will encourage a good flush of autumn flowers.

- RECURRENT-FLOWERING
- FULL SUN
- CAN BE CONTAINER-GROWN
- DISEASE-RESISTANT

'Blue Moon'

History: Considered to be one of the best lilac-flowering hybrid teas, this rose was developed in Germany in 1964 and has never fallen from favour.

Description: 'Blue Moon' is a wonderful rose for gardeners who love flowers in the blue-purple-lavender colour range. It is a vigorous but compact-growing shrub, reaching no more than 75 cm (2½ ft) in height, with attractive bright green foliage. The flower buds are shapely and a shimmering shade of silvery lilac, opening to large, high-centred blooms with petals that range from silvery lilac to lilac-purple. The rose appears more blue on a sunny day, and it is also highly fragrant.

Parentage: 'Sterling Silver' x seedling x seedling

Other names: 'Blue Monday', 'Sissi', 'Tannacht'

Suggested usage: Make a feature of this outstanding rose as the centrepiece of a mixed bed, or mass-plant it for a dramatic effect. Underplant it with catmint and violets.

- RECURRENT-FLOWERING
- FULL SUN
- CAN BE CONTAINER-GROWN
- RELATIVELY DISEASE-FREE

'Charles de Gaulle'

History: Raised by the French breeders Meilland in 1974, and now grown as frequently as other 'blue' roses.

Description: A most attractive shrubby rose, it will grow to 1.3 m (4¼ ft) in the right situation, and has strong, upright stems and excellent, bright green, glossy foliage. The flowers are large and showy, with petals in the soft mauve-blue colour range. The pointed buds are also prized for cutting and, when in flower, this rose exudes a wonderful, rich perfume.

Parentage: ('Sissi' x 'Prelude') x ('Kordes Sondermeldung' x 'Caprice')

Other names: None

Suggested usage: This is a good, healthy rose to use in a flower bed of mixed mauve, purple and lavender annuals and perennials. Plant it near a pathway where its fragrance can be easily enjoyed.

- RECURRENT-FLOWERING
- FULL SUN
- RELATIVELY DISEASE-FREE

'Chicago Peace'

History: Developed as a sport of the famous 'Peace' rose in the United States in 1962.

Description: This rose carries all the major features of its famous parent, varying only in the colour of the flowers. It grows to 1.5 m (5 ft) or even taller with strong, upright stems and a bushy covering of rich green foliage. The flowers are very large and shapely with petals in various shades of yellow to primrose pink, with tonings of warm copper and orange as they mature. It is a great rose for cutting, and also carries a slight wafting fragrance that is most appealing.

Parentage: Sport of 'Peace'

Other names: None

Suggested usage: The strong, upright growth of this hybrid tea means it can be trained around a pillar or against a trellis or fence. It can also be pruned back hard to encourage a more compact shape.

- RECURRENT-FLOWERING
- FULL SUN
- RELATIVELY DISEASE-FREE

'Comtesse Vandal'

History: A dainty, Dutch-bred hybrid tea introduced to gardens in 1932.

Description: One of the older hybrid tea roses, it forms a compact bush no more than 1 m (3 ft) tall when fully grown. The growth habit is bushy, with masses of healthy-looking foliage from early spring right through into the autumn. The flowers are classically high-centred, with pointed, orange buds that open to pinky-apricot flowers that have a slightly darker colouration in the centre. The flowers are also highly scented and perfect for cutting.

Parentage: ('Ophelia' x 'Mrs Aaron Ward') x 'Souvenir de Claudius Pernet'

Other names: None

Suggested usage: This is a wonderful rose for a mixed bed in the warm colour range – yellows, oranges, apricots and even reds, with just a splash of contrasting purple. It can be grown in a pot to great effect.

▨ RECURRENT-FLOWERING
▨ FULL SUN
▨ CAN BE CONTAINER-GROWN
▨ RELATIVELY DISEASE-FREE

'Dainty Maid'

History: Another of the early hybrid teas, developed in Britain in 1940 and grown consistently ever since.

Description: A compact-growing, shrubby rose, it reaches 1 m (3 ft) in height and spreads no more than 60 cm (2 ft). It makes quite strong, upright growth with sturdy stems and masses of very leathery, dark green foliage. The large, beautiful flowers are carried in abundant clusters, opening from pointed buds to single flowers with silvery pink petals that feature a deep pink reverse. The stamens are bright yellow and showy and the overall effect of the plant in flower is exquisite.

Parentage: 'D. T. Poulsen' x unknown seedling

Other names: None

Suggested usage: 'Dainty Maid' is a good, all-round rose for flower beds and borders, or for use as a special container plant for a great flower display in summer. Deadhead spent blooms or use the flowers for cutting.

▨ RECURRENT-FLOWERING
▨ FULL SUN
▨ CAN BE CONTAINER-GROWN
▨ RELATIVELY DISEASE-FREE

'Diamond Jubilee'

History: Bred by the rosarian Boerner in the United States in 1947.

Description: A compact, bushy shrub, it grows to 1 m (3 ft), and has an excellent coverage of dark green, leathery foliage right through the growing season. The showy flowers are large, cup-shaped and fully double, with petals of cream highlighted with shades of apricot. The second flower flush in autumn tends to produce slightly smaller, darker blooms. There is a light fragrance to the flowers and the long, strong stems make it a classic rose for cutting.

Parentage: 'Maréchal Niel' x 'Feu Pernet-Ducher'

Other names: None

Suggested usage: The compact size and shape of this rose make it ideal as a tub specimen – position it in full sun. It can also be mass-planted as a low hedge, producing a never-ending supply of flowers in the summer.

- RECURRENT-FLOWERING
- FULL SUN
- CAN BE CONTAINER-GROWN
- DISEASE-RESISTANT

'Double Delight'

History: An award-winning rose developed in the United States in 1977.

Description: A popular and widely grown bushy shrub, this rose reaches 1 m (3 ft) in height. The foliage is abundant, deep green and glossy and the flowers emerge from pointed, scarlet, urn-shaped buds to reveal pale pink petals edged with strawberry-red, which is a most dramatic combination. The blooms are also strongly fragrant, which adds greatly to this rose's charm. It can be rather problematic to cultivate due to its tendency to develop mildew and other fungal diseases.

Parentage: 'Granada' x 'Garden Party'

Other names: 'Andeli'

Suggested usage: A great feature rose because of its brilliantly contrasting flowers, it can be grown in a container positioned prominently when in full bloom. Take care to water the rose only at ground level.

RECURRENT-FLOWERING

FULL SUN

CAN BE CONTAINER-GROWN

SUSCEPTIBLE TO BLACK SPOT

'Etoile de Hollande'

History: A wonderful, red hybrid tea rose bred in Holland during 1931.

Description: One of the most dramatic of the early, red-flowering hybrid teas, this compact, bushy shrub rose grows to no more than 60 cm (2 ft), and has masses of deep green, matt foliage that provides an excellent setting for the flowers. The flowers are cup-shaped and semi-double with rich red petals and brilliant yellow stamens that become visible as the flower opens. It is seldom cultivated these days – except the climbing form – probably because of its tendency to develop mildew. If the plant remains healthy, the flowers are excellent for cutting.

Parentage: 'General MacArthur' x 'Hadley'

Other names: None

Suggested usage: This rose could be used as a low-growing hedge or as a container rose.

- ▩ RECURRENT-FLOWERING
- ▨ FULL SUN
- ▩ CAN BE CONTAINER-GROWN
- ▩ SUSCEPTIBLE TO BLACK SPOT

'Foster's Melbourne Cup'

History: A New Zealand-bred rose released in 1988, and named in honour of the famous horse race.

Description: An outstanding rose, despite its commercialized name, it is said to rival the famous 'Iceberg' in the quality and quantity of its blooms. It grows to 1.2 m (4 ft) in height, and has an abundance of healthy, mid-green foliage. Each stem carries several large, showy blooms which are a rich shade of golden-yellow. As it opens, each bloom flattens out to reveal decorative yellow stamens, and they are also slightly fragrant, which makes this rose excellent for cutting.

Parentage: 'Sexy Rexy' x 'Pot o' Gold'

Other names: 'Foster's Wellington Cup'

Suggested usage: This is a good rose for a prominent position in a flower bed or border. Regular cutting of the flowers will encourage even more growth.

- ▩ RECURRENT-FLOWERING
- ▨ FULL SUN
- ▩ CAN BE CONTAINER-GROWN
- ▩ RELATIVELY DISEASE-FREE

- RECURRENT-FLOWERING
- FULL SUN
- CAN BE CONTAINER-GROWN
- DISEASE-RESISTANT

'Fragrant Cloud'

History: A New Zealand-bred rose, developed by the expatriate Irish breeder McCredy in 1988.

Description: One of the best roses ever bred in New Zealand, this is a vigorous bush rose that grows to 1 m (3 ft), with lots of healthy, mid-green foliage that seems to be disease-resistant. The flowers are a delight – coral-red with ruffled petals that open to produce a very flat, showy display. The blooms are also sweetly scented, and are wonderful for cutting.

Parentage: 'Sexy Rexy' x 'Pot o' Gold'

Other names: 'Tanellis'

Suggested usage: Prized for the sheer quantity and quality of the petals, this rose is wonderful when mass-planted along a fenceline, creating a continuous display in summer. It can also be pruned back and grown as an excellent container specimen.

'Gold Medal'

History: A reliable hybrid tea rose bred in the United States in 1982, and becoming very popular internationally.

Description: An upright, bushy shrub, it grows to 1.5 m (5 ft), and has strong stems well clothed in large, deep green leaves. The flowers are classic hybrid tea blooms – opening from long, pointed buds to produce high-centred, double blooms with rich golden petals suffused with copper. Although it has only a slight tea fragrance, it is still considered an excellent rose for cutting and is often seen as an exhibition bloom due to its perfect shape.

Parentage: 'Yellow Pages' x ('Granada' x 'Garden Party')

Other names: 'Aroyqueli'

Suggested usage: Plant this rose in a mixed bed of perennials and annuals in the yellow, red and orange colour range. Routinely pick the flowers for arranging indoors, and it will reward you with recurrent flowering.

■ RECURRENT-FLOWERING
▨ FULL SUN
▨ RELATIVELY DISEASE-FREE

'Grandpa Dickson'

History: A classic hybrid tea rose bred in Northern Ireland in 1966 and grown consistently by rose lovers and exhibitors ever since.

Description: A compact yet bushy shrub, it grows to only 75 cm (2½ ft), but produces strong, upright growth and ample, mid-green foliage. The sturdy, thorny stems carry a good crop of large, pale yellow flowers that can be tinged with pink flushes during summer if the weather is particularly warm. This rose flowers prolifically and also produces a light, sweet fragrance that is most appealing.

Parentage: ('Perfecta' x 'Governor Braga da Cruz') x 'Piccadilly'

Other names: 'Irish Gold'

Suggested usage: A charming rose; plant it in the centre of a flower bed or border where its massed flowering can be seen to great effect. It is also compact enough to be grown in a container, placed prominently during the main flowering period.

■ RECURRENT-FLOWERING
▨ FULL SUN
■ CAN BE CONTAINER-GROWN
■ RELATIVELY DISEASE-FREE

'Harry Wheatcroft'

History: An outstanding striped hybrid tea rose developed in Britain in 1972 and later developed in the United States as a climber.

Description: A small but well-shaped shrub, it grows to 75 cm (2½ ft) in height, and has strong, upright stems and a plentiful supply of coppery green, almost glossy foliage. The flowers are perfectly shaped and flamboyantly striped – a background of orange-red with rich yellow markings. The colours of this rose intensify as it matures, and the light fragrance is also appealing.

Parentage: A sport of 'Piccadilly'

Other names: 'Caribia'

Suggested usage: This is a rose to feature prominently because of its outstanding flowers. It is suitable for container cultivation and must have well-drained soil and ground-level watering as it is susceptible to both rust and black spot.

▓ RECURRENT-FLOWERING
▒ FULL SUN
▓ CAN BE CONTAINER-GROWN
▓ SUSCEPTIBLE TO BLACK SPOT

'Helen Traubel'

History: An American-bred rose introduced to gardeners in 1951.

Description: A favourite rose for many years, it is prized for the unusual colour of its flowers. This is a strong-growing rose, reaching 1.5 m (5 ft), with sturdy stems and masses of large, dark green leaves right through the season. The flowers are produced from classic, pointed buds and open quite softly, with warm pinkish apricot petals that fade as they mature. The flowers have a tendency to flop because the neck is sometimes weak, otherwise they are good for cutting because of their delicate perfume.

Parentage: 'Charlotte Armstrong' x 'Glowing Sunset'

Other names: None

Suggested usage: This is a lovely soft rose for a romantic flower border, teamed with annuals and perennials in the yellow, cream and apricot colour range. Routinely deadhead the spent flowers and feed well at the end of summer for a good autumn display.

▓ RECURRENT-FLOWERING
▒ FULL SUN
▓ RELATIVELY DISEASE-FREE

'Ingrid Bergman'

History: Considered to be one of the best red-flowering hybrid teas, bred in Denmark in 1983 and grown consistently ever since.

Description: A vigorous, free-flowering shrub, this rose grows to only 70 cm (2¼ ft), and has a good covering of mid- to dark green, leathery foliage. The strong, upright stems produce large, dark red flowers that are fully double and only slightly fragrant. It is often grown just as a cutting rose because of the long, strong stems and outstanding blooms.

Parentage: 'Precious Platinum' x seedling

Other names: 'Poulman'

Suggested usage: The pure red colour of this rose makes it a perfect accent plant in a mixed bed of warm shades such as yellow, orange and apricot. It can also be grown in a bed of contrasting blues and purples and is small enough to grow in a container.

▓ RECURRENT-FLOWERING
▒ FULL SUN
▓ CAN BE CONTAINER-GROWN
▓ DISEASE-RESISTANT

'Josephine Bruce'

History: Bred in Britain in 1949, there is also a useful climbing form available.

Description: A red-flowering hybrid tea which is highly prized for cutting, the bush form is compact, growing only to 1 m (3 ft). It has thorny stems and excellent, matt green foliage. The large, fragrant flowers are perfectly formed with classic centres and petals in a rich dark red that really stand out on the plant. Although it flowers right through the season, the early summer and autumn flowers are the most outstanding.

Parentage: 'Crimson Glory' x 'Madge Whipp'

Other names: None

Suggested usage: Both the climbing and bush forms are excellent stand-out plants for lovers of red flowers. The bush rose is compact enough to be a perfect container specimen, and the climbing form works well against a fence or trellis. Avoid close underplantings which can create humidity and black spot.

▓ RECURRENT-FLOWERING
▒ FULL SUN
▓ CAN BE CONTAINER-GROWN
▓ SUSCEPTIBLE TO BLACK SPOT

'Julia's Rose'

History: A rose prized for its unusual colouring, bred in Britain in 1976 and still widely grown to this day. There is also a climbing form.

Description: 'Julia's Rose' is a small, compact bush growing to 70 cm (2¼ ft), with upright stem growth. It is clothed in attractive, deep green foliage sometimes tinged with copper highlights. The flowers are small but fully double, in shades of caramel-tan blended with pink highlights. The petal edges are slightly frilled which, together with the unusual colouring, makes it quite a talking point. The flowers are slightly fragrant and excellent for cutting.

Parentage: 'Blue Moon' x 'Dr A. J. Verhage'

Other names: None

Suggested usage: Avoid planting this rose in beds or borders with brightly coloured flowers, which will distract from its unique colouring. It tends to be quite hard to cultivate, but once established it will be most rewarding.

- RECURRENT-FLOWERING
- FULL SUN
- CAN BE CONTAINER-GROWN
- RELATIVELY DISEASE-FREE

'Just Joey'

History: A popular hybrid tea rose developed in Britain in 1972.

Description: The ragged petals of this warmly coloured rose make it look softer than many other hybrid teas and probably explain some of its popularity. It is a moderately vigorous shrub growing to 75 cm (2½ ft) in height, and has only a light covering of deep green foliage. The large flowers are fully double with petals in various shades of fawn, buff-orange and apricot with touches of soft pink at the edges.

Parentage: 'Fragrant Cloud' x 'Dr A. J. Verhage'

Other names: None

Suggested usage: This is a charming rose for the front of a mixed flower border, or for a container positioned in a sunny, open position. It is hardy and reliable.

- RECURRENT-FLOWERING
- FULL SUN
- CAN BE CONTAINER-GROWN
- DISEASE-RESISTANT

'Kardinal'

History: A highly prized, red-flowering hybrid tea rose bred in Germany in 1985.

Description: A robust, free-flowering rose, it grows to 1.2 m (4 ft) in height, and has matt green foliage and long, strong stems that make it ideal for cutting and exhibition. The perfect, pointed buds open to large, bright cardinal-red flowers that are high-centred and velvety. It is often grown commercially for the cut-flower market, and is also a great home garden variety.

Parentage: Seedling x 'Flamingo'

Other names: None

Suggested usage: Mass-plant this rose against a fence or wall for a truly dramatic summer display. It can also be used as a feature plant in a mixed border where it will really stand out against complementary or contrasting colour schemes.

- RECURRENT-FLOWERING
- TOLERATES SOME SHADE
- CAN BE CONTAINER-GROWN
- DISEASE-RESISTANT

'Maria Callas'

History: Named in honour of the famous opera singer, this rose was bred in France in 1965. There is also a climbing form which is equally beautiful.

Description: A medium-sized, bushy shrub, it grows to 1.2 m (4 ft), and has leathery, semi-glossy foliage. The strong stems carry very large, cup-shaped flowers which are generously packed with petals in a rich shade of dark pink. The flowers have a strong, heady fragrance and are wonderful for cutting and exhibition.

Parentage: 'Chrysler Imperial' x 'Karl Herbst'

Other names: 'Miss All American Beauty'

Suggested usage: This rose is sometimes grown as a hedge because of its extra large, prolific flowers. It can also be grown purely for cutting.

- RECURRENT-FLOWERING
- FULL SUN
- RELATIVELY DISEASE-FREE

'Michelle Joy'

History: A rich and warm hybrid tea bred in the United States in 1991.

Description: A tall, upward-growing shrub, it reaches 1.2 m (4 ft), and has a good covering of healthy, mid-green foliage. Classic, pointed buds open to very large, well-shaped, high-centred, double blooms that are pale pink to rich pink in colour. The fragrance is very slight, but it still makes an excellent rose for cutting.

Parentage: Seedling x 'Shreveport'

Other names: 'Aroshrel'

Suggested usage: This is a tremendous background rose for a mixed flower border due to the tall growth and long slender stems that are topped with at least two blooms at a time. It can be pruned back to make a more compact bush.

- RECURRENT-FLOWERING
- FULL SUN
- DISEASE-RESISTANT

RECURRENT-FLOWERING
FULL SUN
RELATIVELY DISEASE-FREE

'Mister Lincoln'

History: The most popular commercially grown red rose for the cut-flower market, bred in the United States in 1964.

Description: This perennial favourite among rose growers for exhibition is quite a small bush, growing to 1 m (3 ft), and has leathery, dull green foliage that belies the beauty of the flowers. Each bloom is carried on a long, strong stem and opens from urn-shaped buds to produce high-centred, cup-shaped blooms of a rich dark red. Part of the appeal of this rose is the way the flowers hold their colour and shape for so long after cutting – and of course, the strong perfume.

Parentage: 'Chrysler Imperial' x 'Charles Mallerin'

Other names: None

Suggested usage: This rose is often grown mass-planted in a flower bed, or just for cutting. The bush itself is rather plain, so it isn't really suited as a centrepiece.

■ RECURRENT-FLOWERING
■ FULL SUN
■ RELATIVELY DISEASE-FREE

'Oklahoma'

History: A slightly different result from the same parentage as 'Mister Lincoln', bred in the United States in 1964.

Description: An award-winning, dark red rose, it isn't as popular, but is possibly more beautiful, than its close relative 'Mister Lincoln'. It is a tall-growing, vigorous bush that reaches 1.2 m (4 ft), and has outstanding, deep green, leathery foliage that makes a good backdrop for the flowers. Each bloom is large and high-centred, with rich velvety red petals and a strong perfume. It is definitely one of the best deep red roses.

Parentage: 'Chrysler Imperial' x 'Charles Mallerin'

Other names: None

Suggested usage: This rose is very versatile as a garden specimen because all aspects of it are attractive. It can be a background rose in a mixed border, or trained against a trellis or fence as a small climber. It is hardy and easy to grow.

'Papa Meilland'

History: Another excellent red rose resulting from the same hybrid cross as 'Oklahoma', developed in France in 1963.

Description: A handsome, upright shrub, it reaches 1 m (3 ft) in height, and has plenty of leathery, olive-green foliage that is slightly glossy, as well as sturdy stems that are somewhat thorny and inhospitable. The flowers, however, are a joy – large and well shaped with velvety, deep crimson petals and a strong, heady fragrance. It is excellent as a cut flower or as an exhibition bloom.

Parentage: 'Chrysler Imperial' x 'Charles Mallerin'

Other names: 'Meisar'

Suggested usage: This rose needs a sunny and well-ventilated position to thrive, due to its susceptibility to fungal diseases – especially mildew. Therefore, plant it as a lone specimen and water only at ground level.

■ RECURRENT-FLOWERING
■ FULL SUN
■ CAN BE CONTAINER-GROWN
■ SUSCEPTIBLE TO BLACK SPOT

'Pascali'

History: Bred in Belgium in 1963, this rose was highly prized in its day, winning several international gold medals.

Description: Still popular after nearly 40 years, this is one of the best white roses for the home gardener. It is a compact shrub, seldom more than 1 m (3 ft) in height, with healthy mid-green foliage and quite strong, upright stems. The flowers are beautifully shaped and almost pure white, with a soft cream base. The fragrance is only slight, yet the blooms make wonderful cut flowers because of their size and shape.

Parentage: 'Queen Elizabeth' x 'White Butterfly'

Other names: 'Blanche Pasca'

Suggested usage: Plant this rose in a bed of cream- and white-flowering annuals and perennials, in a position which can be enjoyed at dusk – the peak time of day for viewing white flowers.

- RECURRENT-FLOWERING
- TOLERATES SOME SHADE
- CAN BE CONTAINER-GROWN
- DISEASE-RESISTANT

'Peace'

History: Perhaps the most famous of all hybrid teas, bred in France in 1945 and still widely grown all over the world. There is also a climbing form.

Description: A multi award-winning rose, it has many virtues and is a must for any serious rose grower. The bush form grows to 1.4 m (4½ ft), and is vigorous, with masses of glossy, deep green foliage. The lightly fragrant flowers are outstanding. Large and perfectly formed, they are bright yellow flushed with red-pink around the edges. The buds are plump and golden-yellow and the overall effect when in flower is glorious.

Parentage: ('George Dickson' x 'Souvenir de Claudius Pernet') x ('Joanna Hill' x 'Charles P. Kilham') x 'Margaret McGredy'

Other names: 'Gloria Dei', 'Mme A. Meilland'

Suggested usage: This rose looks great mass-planted or hedged. It makes an ideal centrepiece in a mixed bed, or it can be grown alone as a specimen with great impact.

- RECURRENT-FLOWERING
- FULL SUN
- CAN BE CONTAINER-GROWN
- DISEASE-RESISTANT

'Peter Frankenfeld'

History: A good cutting rose that was developed in Germany in 1966 and has remained popular ever since. There is also an attractive climbing form.

Description: Growing to 1.3 m (4¼ ft) in height, it has masses of glossy green foliage and a compact, bushy form that is most attractive. The flowers, which are abundant right through the growing season, are carried on long, strong stems, each opening from a pointed bud to produce well-shaped, high-centred blooms with a light but fresh fragrance. The deep pink flowers are considered good for cutting because they hold their shape and colour for a long time.

Parentage: Unrecorded

Other names: None

Suggested usage: The overall good appearance of this rose makes it suitable for use in a perennial border or as a medium-sized hedge against a fenceline. It is a good all-rounder.

- RECURRENT-FLOWERING
- FULL SUN
- RELATIVELY DISEASE-FREE

■ RECURRENT-FLOWERING
■ FULL SUN
■ CAN BE CONTAINER-GROWN
■ DISEASE-RESISTANT

'Precious Platinum'

History: A worthwhile, red-flowering hybrid tea rose developed in Northern Ireland in 1974.

Description: A vigorous, upright shrub, it grows to 1 m (3 ft) in height, and has plenty of leathery, dark green foliage which serves as a backdrop to the flowers. The prolific blooms are carried on long, strong stems, opening as high-centred, very double flowers with wonderfully rich, cardinal-red petals The flowers are lightly fragrant and therefore fantastic for cutting or exhibition. This is an easy rose for the beginner.

Parentage: 'Red Planet' x 'Franklin Englemann'

Other names: 'Opa Potschke', 'Red Star'

Suggested usage: 'Precious Platinum' is a useful rose for its ease of cultivation and its tolerance of poorer soils. It can be used as a low hedge, mass-planted in a bed or grown as an accent plant for its rich red blooms.

'Princesse de Monaco'

History: Named in honour of the actress Grace Kelly, this perennial favourite was bred in France in 1982.

Description: Very similar to its parent the 'Peace' rose, this reliable rose has stronger and more upright growth. The stems carry an abundance of large, dark green, glossy foliage and the overall shape of the shrub, which grows to 1.2 m (4 ft), is desirable. The large and perfectly formed, creamy flowers have petals edged in pink, and they are prized as cut flowers and for exhibition. They have the added bonus of a delightful, light fragrance.

Parentage: 'Ambassador' x 'Peace'

Other names: 'Princess Grace'

Suggested usage: A rose that looks good right through the growing season, it can be used as a feature in a mixed flower bed or rose border. Cut the blooms routinely to encourage new growth of flowering stems.

- RECURRENT-FLOWERING
- FULL SUN
- CAN BE CONTAINER-GROWN
- RELATIVELY DISEASE-FREE

'Princess Margaret'

History: Developed in France it 1968, this rose has remained a firm favourite with both gardeners and rose exhibitors. There is also a climbing variety.

Description: An easy-to-grow and reliable garden favourite, it is valued for its shapely flowers and disease resistance. Growing to only 75 cm (2½ ft) in height, it forms a compact bush of leathery, dark green foliage. The fragrant flowers are large and showy, carried on long, strong stems, with petals in a rich shade of phlox-pink that hold their colour and form for many days after cutting.

Parentage: 'Queen Elizabeth' x ('Peace' x 'Michèle Meilland')

Other names: 'Meilista'

Suggested usage: A useful rose for a mixed flower bed, it can be combined with annuals and perennials in the pink, white and purple colour range to great effect. Regular picking encourages more flowering.

■ RECURRENT-FLOWERING
▨ FULL SUN
▨ CAN BE CONTAINER-GROWN
▨ DISEASE-RESISTANT

'Pristine'

History: An American-bred rose from the late 1970s, prized for its attractive shape and free-flowering habit.

Description: A compact shrub growing to 1 m (3 ft), it has upright stems and masses of dense, deep green foliage right through the growing season. The flowers are very large and showy and are produced on long, strong stems that are ideal for cutting. Each bloom is lightly fragrant with nearly white petals shaded in pink. 'Pristine' makes a good cut flower, and performs better in spring than in summer.

Parentage: 'White Masterpiece' x 'First Prize'

Other names: 'Jacpico'

Suggested usage: A healthy and easy to cultivate rose, it will give good results, even to the beginner. Plant it as a low hedge, or grow it in a large container positioned prominently for a late-spring display.

■ RECURRENT-FLOWERING
▨ FULL SUN
▨ CAN BE CONTAINER-GROWN
▨ DISEASE-RESISTANT

'Red Devil'

History: An American-bred hybrid tea rose introduced to gardeners in 1970.

Description: A strong-growing, bushy plant, it reaches 1.2 m (4 ft) in height and has upright stems and masses of glossy, bright green foliage. The pretty buds open to fully double, well-shaped blooms that are a warm mid-red colour, slightly lighter on the reverse. The flowers have an excellent scent and are perfect for picking, although heavy rain will spoil their appearance. Ideally, they need a climate with a hot, dry summer.

Parentage: 'Silver Lining' x 'Prima Ballerina' seedling

Other names: 'Coeur d'Amour'

Suggested usage: Position this rose in a bed of hot-coloured flowers – reds, yellows and oranges – with just a splash of blue or purple as a contrast. Always plant it in full sun to maximize the beauty of the flowers.

RECURRENT-FLOWERING
FULL SUN
RELATIVELY DISEASE-FREE

'Royal Dane'

History: A handsome rose in the orange colour range, bred in Denmark in 1971 and still popular with gardeners.

Description: A compact but vigorous shrub, it grows to 75 cm (2½ ft), and has a good covering of dark green, glossy foliage. The perfectly shaped flowers are carried on long, strong stems, each bloom opening from a dark orange bud to a classic, high-centred, double flower in delightful shades of pink and yellow-orange. This is a popular rose with exhibitors, and is perfect for cutting.

Parentage: ('Super Star' x 'Baccara') x ('Princess Astrid' x 'Hanne')

Other names: 'Troika'

Suggested usage: A compact rose, it is ideal for container cultivation. Select a large pot and plant three together for a fantastic, non-stop summer display – you'll have plenty of roses for the house as well.

- RECURRENT-FLOWERING
- FULL SUN
- CAN BE CONTAINER-GROWN
- RELATIVELY DISEASE-FREE

RECURRENT-FLOWERING
FULL SUN
CAN BE CONTAINER-GROWN
RELATIVELY DISEASE-FREE

'Sexy Rexy'

History: A New Zealand-bred rose, released in 1984, with rather a silly name that may turn some gardeners off – which is a shame, as it is beautiful.

Description: A compact, bushy shrub, it grows to 1 m (3 ft) in height, and has vigorous, upright stems and small, light green foliage that is glossy and healthy through the season. The flowers are prolific and carried in clusters, and are large and very double with a camellia-like appearance. The soft pink blooms have a delightful fragrance and are ideal for cutting. This rose needs extra fertilizing to perform well.

Parentage: 'Seaspray' x 'Dreaming'

Other names: 'Macrexy'

Suggested usage: This is a versatile rose than can be mass-planted, used as a low hedge or planted in a container. Regular deadheading of the spent blooms will encourage more flowering.

- RECURRENT-FLOWERING
- FULL SUN
- CAN BE CONTAINER-GROWN
- DISEASE-RESISTANT

'Shot Silk'

History: A very old and beautiful hybrid tea rose developed in Northern Ireland in 1924 and still prized by rose lovers.

Description: Considered to be one of the best roses of its day, 'Shot Silk' has stood the test of time. It is a very small, compact and bushy shrub that grows to 50 cm (1¾ ft), and has luxuriant, glossy foliage that remains healthy right through the season. It is very free-flowering, with full, high-centred flowers that are a mixture of pink, salmon, orange and yellow, with a wonderful sheen to the petals – which inspired the name. It has a delicate fragrance and is perfect for cutting.

Parentage: 'Hugh Dickson' seedling x 'Sunstar'

Other names: None

Suggested usage: Lovers of old roses will enjoy adding this to their collection. It makes a most attractive container rose, and can be kept compact with routine trimming back and deadheading.

'Silver Jubilee'

History: Bred in Scotland in 1978, this is yet another perennial favourite prized for its cutting qualities.

Description: This rose produces a well-shaped, bushy shrub to 1 m (3 ft) in height, and has glossy, mid-green foliage that is a good backdrop for the flowers. The showy blooms are very large and perfectly formed, with petals that are a delightful blend of salmon-pink and apricot with a deeper reverse. They are also sweetly perfumed, which adds to the beauty of the plant.

Parentage: ('Highlight' x 'Colour Wonder') x (Parkdirektor Riggers' x 'Piccadilly') x 'Mischief'

Other names: None

Suggested usage: 'Silver Jubilee' is a pretty rose for a mixed bed or border, planted with annuals and perennials in the yellow, orange and apricot colour range. It can also be grown in a container.

- RECURRENT-FLOWERING
- FULL SUN
- CAN BE CONTAINER-GROWN
- RELATIVELY DISEASE-FREE

'Silver Lining'

History: An English-bred rose dating back to 1958, but still highly prized for the beauty of its blooms.

Description: A compact, bushy shrub, it grows to 60 cm (2 ft) in height and spreads to about the same width. The stems are strong and upright, covered in thorns, and the foliage is small, matt green and rather sparse. The high-centred flowers make up for this deficiency, though. Large and exquisitely shaped, they are a soft blush-rose with deep pink highlights and a soft fragrance that makes them irresistible.

Parentage: 'Karl Herbst' x 'Eden Rose'

Other names: None

Suggested usage: A wonderful rose for a container, positioned prominently during the main growing season. Routine cutting of the flowers, or deadheading of the spent blooms, encourages new growth.

- RECURRENT-FLOWERING
- FULL SUN
- CAN BE CONTAINER-GROWN
- RELATIVELY DISEASE-FREE

'Sonia'

History: Bred in France by Meilland in 1974, there is also a climbing sport which is most worthwhile.

Description: A dense and bushy shrub, it grows to 75 cm (2½ ft), and has upright stems and deep green, leathery foliage that makes a good backdrop for the flowers. Long, pointed buds open to semi-double blooms that are rosette-shaped with pale pink petals that are suffused with coral. It has a light, fruity fragrance that is most appealing. Heavy rain will spoil the flowers.

Parentage: 'Zambra' x ('Baccara' x 'Message')

Other names: 'Sweet Promise'

Suggested usage: A pretty, compact rose, it is great for growing in a container, or for edging a rose bed as a low, flower-filled hedge. Extra fertilizing will improve flowering results.

- RECURRENT-FLOWERING
- FULL SUN
- CAN BE CONTAINER-GROWN
- SUSCEPTIBLE TO BLACK SPOT

'Virgo'

History: Bred in France in 1947, this charming old hybrid tea rose is a perennial favourite for the garden.

Description: A slender, upright-growing shrub that grows to 75 cm (2½ ft), it has a good covering of healthy, mid-green foliage. The flowers are the main attraction. Opening loosely from shapely, pointed buds, the blooms have pure white petals that hold their colour for a long period. The flowers are carried on strong stems and have a sweet fragrance, which makes them ideal for cutting.

Parentage: 'Blanche Mallerin' x 'Neige Parfum'

Other names: None

Suggested usage: This is an excellent white rose for a monochromatic white border, planted with complementary annuals and perennials. It can also be grown in a container, and should be routinely deadheaded to encourage new growth.

- RECURRENT-FLOWERING
- FULL SUN
- CAN BE CONTAINER-GROWN
- RELATIVELY DISEASE-FREE

FLORIBUNDA
ROSES

These charming modern hybrid roses are also known as 'cluster-flowered' roses, because they carry their flowers in large sprays or clusters, making them very showy and attractive. The first floribundas were developed in Holland in 1924 as the result of a cross between a hybrid tea rose and a polyantha rose. The result was a compact shrub with very large clusters of flowers that bloomed recurrently right through the summer. Initially floribundas were bred only in various shades of pink and red. However, in the 1930s a yellow rose was introduced, and these days floribundas are being produced in a wider range of colours including apricots, pure white and even 'hand-painted' varieties that are multicoloured. Perhaps the most famous floribunda is 'Iceberg', which is probably the world's best loved and most commonly grown white-flowering rose.

PREVIOUS PAGE 'Brass Band'

'Amber Queen'

History: A rose developed by the English breeder Harkness in 1984.

Description: 'Amber Queen' is a compact and bushy shrub, growing to 60 cm (2 ft) in height, with masses of rather large leaves that are deep green with a maroon tinge. The flowers are very large and showy, and carried in clusters. Each bloom is fully double with amber-yellow petals and a strong, heady fragrance which adds to the appeal. In time the bush will develop a very attractive spreading habit.

Parentage: 'Southampton' x 'Typhoon'

Other names: 'Prinz Eugen von Savoyen'

Suggested usage: This is an excellent rose to include in a mixed border where yellows, oranges and reds are included in the colour scheme. It can also be used as a low hedge if it is routinely deadheaded and shaped.

- RECURRENT-FLOWERING
- FULL SUN
- CAN BE CONTAINER-GROWN
- RELATIVELY DISEASE-FREE

'Apricot Nectar'

History: An American-bred floribunda rose introduced in 1965, it has remained popular all around the world ever since.

Description: This is a handsome, compact shrub that generally reaches 70 cm (2¼ ft) in height, with a good covering of pale green foliage and masses of strong, upward-growing stems. The flowers are large and rounded in shape, with soft apricot petals that are tinged with pink. The flowers are also well scented and are ideal for cutting and exhibition.

Parentage: Seedling x 'Spartan'

Other names: None

Suggested usage: Make a feature of this rose, which will reward with prolific flowering right through the season. If kept well pruned, it is compact enough for container cultivation.

- RECURRENT-FLOWERING
- FULL SUN
- CAN BE CONTAINER-GROWN
- RELATIVELY DISEASE-FREE

'Bridal Pink'

History: A charming American-bred, cluster-flowered floribunda, introduced to gardens in 1967.

Description: Popular for decades as a rose for bridal bouquets, this large-growing shrub reaches 1.2 m (4 ft) in height, and has vigorous stem growth and excellent, leathery, deep green leaves. The flowers are medium-sized, opening from pale pink buds to produce high-centred, double flowers with white petals lightly blushed with pale pink. The blooms are highly fragrant, which adds to their appeal.

Parentage: 'Summertime' x 'Spartan'

Other names: None

Suggested usage: This is a wonderful rose to include in a border or bed of white or pastel flowers. Routine cutting will encourage more flower production and keep the shrub looking tidy.

- RECURRENT-FLOWERING
- FULL SUN
- CAN BE CONTAINER-GROWN
- RELATIVELY DISEASE-FREE

'Colour Break'

History: A very striking and unusual New Zealand-bred floribunda, available to gardeners since 1982.

Description: An outstanding variety, this grows to 1 m (3 ft) in height, and has healthy and luxuriant, glossy, deep green foliage right through the season. The flowers are large and fully double, with deep reddish orange petals that have a brownish hue, especially when the weather is cool. The buds and flowers together are most attractive and are prized for cutting and exhibition, both for their colouring and perfect shape.

Parentage: 'Mary Sumner' x 'Kapai'

Other names: 'Brown Velvet'

Suggested usage: A hedge of this unusual rose can be a real talking point in the garden. If pruned, 'Colour Break' can also be grown in a container, or combined with other hot colours in a mixed flower bed.

- ▨ RECURRENT-FLOWERING
- ▨ FULL SUN
- ▨ CAN BE CONTAINER-GROWN
- ▨ RELATIVELY DISEASE-FREE

'Europeana'

History: A truly beautiful, red-flowering floribunda bred in Holland in 1963, and still a popular shrub with home gardeners.

Description: The tremendously appealing combination of glossy foliage and brilliant crimson flowers is seen at its best with this rose variety. Growing to only 60 cm (2 ft) in height, it is a vigorous, almost thornless bush with reddish green foliage which acts as a perfect backdrop for the flowers. Each bloom is large and double, with deep crimson-red petals and a light but appealing fragrance. It is a hard rose to beat.

Parentage: 'Ruth Leuwerik' x 'Rosemary Rose'

Other names: None

Suggested usage: This is an excellent hedging rose, although it will appear bedraggled during rainfall as the flower trusses are so large and heavily laden. Keep the base of the plant weed-free to prevent mildew.

- ▨ RECURRENT-FLOWERING
- ▨ FULL SUN
- ▨ CAN BE CONTAINER-GROWN
- ▨ SUSCEPTIBLE TO BLACK SPOT

'French Lace'

History: A delightful floribunda rose bred in the United States in 1980.

Description: A compact and bushy shrub growing to 1.2 m (4 ft), it has a good covering of small, dark green leaves that should remain healthy right through the growing season. The flowers are carried in large clusters, opening from pointed buds to produce double blooms in a wonderful shade of ivory-white with an apricot blush as they mature. The blooms have a light, fruity fragrance and are wonderful for cutting or for bouquets.

Parentage: 'Dr. A. J. Verhage' x 'Bridal Pink'

Other names: 'Jaclace'

Suggested usage: This is a reliable rose for a mixed flower bed or border, and produces blooms right through the season. Routine deadheading will improve the flowering.

- RECURRENT-FLOWERING
- FULL SUN
- CAN BE CONTAINER-GROWN
- RELATIVELY DISEASE-FREE

'Friesia'

History: A charming cluster-flowered floribunda bred in Germany in 1974.

Description: Growing to 75 cm (2½ ft) in height, this floribunda variety forms a neat, bushy shrub with a good covering of healthy, light green foliage. The flowers are large and showy, opening to a loose, flat shape with the clearest of yellow petals and a strong fragrance. This rose is prized for its reliable flowering, even in relatively poor growing conditions.

Parentage: 'Friedrich Wörlein' x 'Spanish Sun'

Other names: 'Korresia', 'Sunsprite'

Suggested usage: This vigorous, tough rose can be grown in a vast range of climates and conditions. The bright yellow blooms look good when contrasted against blue- or purple-flowering annuals and perennials.

- RECURRENT-FLOWERING
- TOLERATES SOME SHADE
- CAN BE CONTAINER-GROWN
- RELATIVELY DISEASE-FREE

'Gold Bunny'

History: A charming cluster-flowered floribunda developed in France in 1978.

Description: A well-formed, compact shrub, it grows to 70 cm (2¼ ft), and has a good covering of light green foliage that, unfortunately, is prone to black spot in humid climates. However, the flowers are outstanding – large and full with clear yellow petals carried in showy clusters right through the season. The blooms also have a light fragrance.

Parentage: 'Poppy Flash' x ('Charlston' x 'Allgold')

Other names: 'Gold Badge'

Suggested usage: This is a lovely yellow rose for a sunny, well-ventilated border, or for growing against a fence as a colourful hedge. Deadhead routinely to encourage ongoing flowering.

- RECURRENT-FLOWERING
- FULL SUN
- CAN BE CONTAINER-GROWN
- SUSCEPTIBLE TO BLACK SPOT

'Gruss an Aachen'

History: A very old and reliable German-bred floribunda, developed from a hybrid perpetual and introduced in 1909.

Description: A bushy, low-growing shrub, it reaches 70 cm (2¼ ft) in height, and has a good covering of matt, mid-green foliage. The flowers have a wonderful old-fashioned quality, being softly cup-shaped with pale creamy white flowers that feature pale pink and peach highlights. The flower clusters are dense with blooms, making this a very showy rose for cutting. It also has a gentle and appealing fragrance.

Parentage: 'Frau Karl Druschki' x 'Franz Deegen'

Other names: None

Suggested usage: This is a perfect floribunda for an old-fashioned or cottage garden, especially when underplanted with spring bulbs and summer annuals.

- RECURRENT-FLOWERING
- FULL SUN
- CAN BE CONTAINER-GROWN
- RELATIVELY DISEASE-FREE

'Iceberg'

Occasionally a rose is produced that captures the hearts of the gardening public – and 'Iceberg' is certainly one of those special varieties. With its soft white or pale pink blooms, it will flower reliably right through the season.

'Iceberg' is an outstanding, white-flowering floribunda, developed by Kordes in Germany in 1958 from 'Robin Hood' x 'Virgo'. It is also known as 'Schneewittchen' or 'Fée des Neiges'. It is an upright, well-shaped shrub rose that grows to 1 m (3 ft) in height, with large, shiny leaves that are glossy and clear green, which therefore provide a perfect backdrop to the white flowers.

'Iceberg' roses are very free-flowering, producing clusters of medium-sized, rounded and double flowers with soft white petals that are sometimes flushed with pale pink. The blooms are highly fragrant and therefore excellent for cutting. More recently a deep pink form has been developed, known as 'Pink Iceberg', which is proving to be almost as prized as the original white.

Expert growers advise not to overfeed 'Iceberg', or it will tend to produce leggy stem growth and foliage at the expense of flowering. Therefore a slow and steady supply of organic matter, breaking down around the base of the bush, will probably be the best approach – with some extra rose fertilizer in spring and late summer to boost flower production.

'Iceberg' is often mass-planted, which is the most effective way to display its charms. Try it in rows to line a driveway or at the back of a garden bed. It is available as a bush, but there are also standards, weeping standards and climbing varieties available.

Despite its beauty, 'Iceberg' is not a rose that is totally without fault, as it is slightly prone to black spot during humid or wet spells. But it is worth the effort as it does produce an almost non-stop display of blooms. To combat black spot, try to position 'Iceberg' so it has plenty of air circulation around it to prevent humidity. The standard form is best in this respect, and looks wonderful in a large tub.

▦ TOLERATES SOME SHADE
▦ SUSCEPTIBLE TO BLACK SPOT
▦ CAN BE CONTAINER-GROWN

ABOVE LEFT 'Iceberg'
OPPOSITE 'Pink Iceberg'

'Iced Ginger'

History: A charming cluster-flowered floribunda introduced by Northern Irish breeders in 1971.

Description: This is a popular variety because of the size and unusual colouration of the blooms, which are among the largest within the floribunda group. Growing to 1 m (3 ft) in height, the bush is rather lanky and open in habit, with mid-green, heavily veined foliage that has reddish highlights. The flowers are produced in large and showy clusters, opening from pointed buds to well-shaped blooms with petals that are a blend of pale pink and ivory with a copper reverse. The flowers are only slightly fragrant but still perfect for cutting.

Parentage: 'Anne Watkins' x seedling

Other names: None

Suggested usage: A reliable floribunda for a mixed flower bed or border, it responds well to regular pruning and deadheading, which helps to maintain a more compact shape and overcomes some of the lankiness.

■ RECURRENT-FLOWERING
▨ FULL SUN
■ CAN BE CONTAINER-GROWN
■ RELATIVELY DISEASE-FREE

'Lavender Pinocchio'

History: An American-bred floribunda, raised in 1948 and still widely grown for its unusual colouring, it has been used extensively for breeding brownish flowers.

Description: This rose broke new ground in colouring, introducing shades of brown never before seen. It is a bushy, robust shrub that is only 60 cm (2 ft) in height, but still very striking. The foliage is leathery and mid-green in colour, and the flowers are produced in showy trusses, each one large and fully double in various shades of pink, lavender and soft brown. It is well scented and very good for cutting.

Parentage: 'Pinocchio' x 'Grey Pearl'

Other names: None

Suggested usage: This is a rose to use as a feature because of its unusual colouring. Plant it in a bed where other coloured flowers won't detract from its charm.

■ RECURRENT-FLOWERING
▨ FULL SUN
■ CAN BE CONTAINER-GROWN
■ RELATIVELY DISEASE-FREE

'Marlena'

History: A German-bred floribunda introduced in 1964 and still widely admired for its red and crimson flowers.

Description: This is a very small-growing rose – almost a miniature in size – reaching no more than 45 cm (1½ ft) at maturity. However, it has a bushy and compact growth habit and very good-quality, dark green foliage that acts as a perfect backdrop for the flowers. For the size of the plant, the flowers are large, opening to semi-double, flat blooms with red and crimson petals and soft yellow stamens.

Parentage: 'Gertrud Westphal' x 'Lilli Marlene'

Other names: None

Suggested usage: 'Marlena' is a perfect rose for a container. Position it prominently in a sunny spot when it is in full flower. It can also be planted as a low hedge at the front of a rose bed.

- ▓ RECURRENT-FLOWERING
- ▒ FULL SUN
- ▓ CAN BE CONTAINER-GROWN
- ▓ RELATIVELY DISEASE-FREE

'New Year'

History: A charming cluster-flowered floribunda, bred by the expatriate Irish rosarian McGredy in New Zealand in 1982.

Description: The beautifully shaped flowers of this floribunda are its main appeal. It is a vigorous shrub, growing to 1.2 m (4 ft) in height, with upright stems clothed in glossy, deep green foliage. The flowers are carried in large clusters, each one perfectly formed with petals in rich shades of orange and gold, creating an overall coppery effect. The blooms are slightly fragrant and perfect for cutting.

Parentage: 'Mary Sumner' x seedling

Other names: 'Arcadian'

Suggested usage: A pretty, warm-toned rose, it is ideal for a bed of orange, yellow and apricot flowers. Plant several close together for a really arresting effect.

- RECURRENT-FLOWERING
- FULL SUN
- CAN BE CONTAINER-GROWN
- RELATIVELY DISEASE-FREE

'Pink Parfait'

History: A soft and pretty American-bred floribunda introduced to gardens in 1960.

Description: A neat and bushy shrub, it grows to 1 m (3 ft) in height, and develops a good, rounded shape. The foliage is semi-glossy and leathery and tends to remain healthy and lush right through the season. The flowers start out as shapely buds then open to large, semi-double blooms with petals in a warm mix of rose-pink, salmon, apricot and peach. They fade to a paler pink as the rose ages, and produce a slight fragrance during warm weather. This is a highly prized floribunda.

Parentage: 'First Love' x 'Pinocchio'

Other names: None

Suggested usage: This rose can be used for hedging or mass-planting, and will perform well and remain healthy right through the summer.

- RECURRENT-FLOWERING
- FULL SUN
- CAN BE CONTAINER-GROWN
- DISEASE-RESISTANT

'Queen Elizabeth'

History: Considered the best ever pink-flowering floribunda, raised in the United States in 1954 and still grown extensively for cutting and exhibition. It was bred to coincide with the coronation of Queen Elizabeth II.

Description: A very tall-growing rose with sturdy stems, it can reach 2 m (6½ ft) or more in height, and has glossy, deep green foliage right through the season. The large flowers are produced in showy clusters, opening from shapely buds to high-centred, clear cyclamen-pink flowers that are slightly fragrant and perfect for cutting.

Parentage: 'Charlotte Armstrong' x 'Floradora'

Other names: 'The Queen Elizabeth Rose'

Suggested usage: This rose needs space to grow well, and will benefit from hard pruning back to prevent those upright stems growing too tall. It can be grown beside an elevated deck where the flowers can be appreciated at an accessible height.

- RECURRENT-FLOWERING
- FULL SUN
- CAN BE CONTAINER-GROWN
- DISEASE-RESISTANT

'Regensberg'

History: Another beautiful New Zealand-bred floribunda, introduced by the expatriate Irish breeder McGredy in 1979.

Description: This is an outstanding variety that is extremely small and compact, growing to just 45 cm (1½ ft) in height, with a plentiful covering of mid-green foliage. It has a tendency to spread during midsummer, producing large clusters of double, pink flowers which are edged with white and also have white on the reverse of the petals, giving a two-toned effect. The flowers are highly fragrant and delightful for cutting.

Parentage: 'Geoff Boycott' x 'Old Master'

Other names: 'Buffalo Bill', 'Young Mistress'

Suggested usage: Use 'Regensberg' as a feature rose because of its unusual flowers. It is also ideal as a container rose, placed in a sunny, open position, or as a low hedging rose along the front of a border.

- RECURRENT-FLOWERING
- FULL SUN
- CAN BE CONTAINER-GROWN
- RELATIVELY DISEASE-FREE

'Scarlet Queen Elizabeth'

History: A red variation of the famous pink 'Queen Elizabeth', developed in Northern Ireland in 1963.

Description: A glorious variation of an old theme, this upright, vigorous floribunda will reach 1.2 m (4 ft) in height, and is therefore not as tall and rangy as its parent plant. However the foliage is just as lush, leathery and deep green and the flowers are carried in large, showy clusters. Each bloom is globular in shape and double, with scarlet petals and a light but delightful fragrance.

Parentage: ('Korona' x seedling) x 'Queen Elizabeth'

Other names: None

Suggested usage: A good all-rounder, this floribunda is perfect for gardeners who love rich red flowers. It can be mass-planted or incorporated into a mixed flower border. Position it anywhere that gets lots of sun.

- RECURRENT-FLOWERING
- FULL SUN
- RELATIVELY DISEASE-FREE

'Shocking Blue'

History: Developed in Germany in 1974, the incorporation of the word 'blue' in the name is attributed to the mauve tint of the blooms.

Description: Not a true blue rose, but a magenta colour with mauve overtones, it is a bushy shrub that reaches 1.2 m (4 ft) in height. It has lush, mid-green foliage and very pretty, pointed flower buds. The flowers are large and double, with mauve-tinted petals and a wonderfully rich perfume that makes them a delight for cutting. This rose is still very popular as an exhibition bloom because of the perfect shape of the flowers.

Parentage: Unknown

Other names: None

Suggested usage: 'Shocking Blue' is a good, reliable rose for any collection, with healthy foliage and prolific flowers right through the season. Combine it with other pink- and white-flowering varieties.

- RECURRENT-FLOWERING
- FULL SUN
- CAN BE CONTAINER-GROWN
- RELATIVELY DISEASE-FREE

'Woburn Abbey'

History: An English-bred, cluster-flowered floribunda introduced in 1962 and still popular with gardeners and growers.

Description: A vigorous and upright shrub, it grows to 1 m (3 ft) or more in height, and has masses of small, dark, shiny leaves that set off the beauty of the flowers. The flowers are produced in small but prolific clusters, each bloom opening from a tight bud to an open, loosely formed rose with golden-orange petals. This is a very striking rose, and it is also fragrant.

Parentage: 'Masquerade' x 'Fashion'

Other names: None

Suggested usage: Mass-plant 'Woburn Abbey' for a truly dramatic impact, especially if you love strong colour schemes. Always plant it in a sunny, well-ventilated position as it is prone to rust.

■ RECURRENT-FLOWERING
■ TOLERATES SOME SHADE
■ SUSCEPTIBLE TO BLACK SPOT
■ CAN BE CONTAINER-GROWN

■ RECURRENT-FLOWERING
▨ FULL SUN
▨ CAN BE CONTAINER-GROWN
■ RELATIVELY DISEASE-FREE

'Zonta Rose'

History: A vivid floribunda developed in Britain in 1985.

Description: A very colourful rose, both in flower and foliage, it is upright and vigorous, growing to 1 m (3 ft) or more in height, and has masses of healthy, bright green foliage. The flowers are carried in large clusters on strong stems that are ideal for cutting. Each bloom is open and semi-double, with clear yellow petals and pretty yellow stamens in the centre. It is highly prized as an exhibition bloom.

Parentage: 'Judy Garland' x 'Anne Harkness'

Other names: 'Bright Lights', 'Princess Alice'

Suggested usage: This is a very worthwhile hedging rose because of its upright growth. The flowers even tolerate bad weather.

SHRUB
ROSES

This category of rose is a bit of a hotch-potch of varieties that don't neatly fit into any of the other hybrid groups. They don't have the obvious characteristics of the hybrid tea rose – tall, straight flower stems, pointed buds and high-centred blooms – or the popular floribundas – flowers carried in clusters or trusses – yet they have plenty to offer the home gardener. Some are suitable for hedging or mass-planting for a dramatic floral effect; some can be used as border plants or for planting against a sunny wall; and some are small enough to grow in containers. Like most roses, they like a sunny, open position with good air circulation and plenty of summer feeding to encourage continuous blooms.

PREVIOUS PAGE 'Lavender Dream'

'Bonica '82'

History: A modern shrub rose bred by Meilland in France in 1982.

Description: This is a compact yet bushy shrub that grows and spreads to 1 m (3 ft). It forms a rounded bush, and has a mass of small, dark green leaves that are semi-glossy and most attractive. The flowers are produced in very large and showy clusters, each bloom being double with bright pink petals that fade slightly as the rose matures. The petals have soft, wavy edges that add greatly to their appeal.

Parentage: (*R. sempervirens* x 'Mlle Marthe Carron') x 'Picasso'

Other names: 'Meidomonac'

Suggested usage: A versatile rose, it is disease-resistant and flowers for long periods, and is ideal as the centrepiece of a mixed pastel border that includes lilac, pink, white and cream annuals and perennials.

- RECURRENT-FLOWERING
- FULL SUN
- CAN BE CONTAINER-GROWN
- RELATIVELY DISEASE-FREE

'Buff Beauty'

History: A very popular hybrid musk rose bred in Britain in 1939 and grown consistently ever since.

Description: A vigorous rose, 'Buff Beauty' is prized for its wonderful shape and the fact that it flowers almost continuously right through the season. Growing and spreading to 1.5 m (5 ft), it forms a lovely mound of copper-tinged, deep green foliage that is topped by large and showy trusses of sweetly fragrant, double flowers. The flowers vary in colour from apricot and rich gold through to warm yellow, depending on the growing environment.

Parentage: Possibly a seedling of 'William Allen Richardson'

Other names: None

Suggested usage: This is a wonderful shrub rose for hedging or planting as the centrepiece of a mixed flower border. It is hardy and adaptable to a wide range of soils and climates, and responds well to quite vigorous pruning.

■ RECURRENT-FLOWERING
■ TOLERATES SOME SHADE
■ RELATIVELY DISEASE-FREE

■ RECURRENT-FLOWERING
□ TOLERATES SOME SHADE
■ RELATIVELY DISEASE-FREE

'Elmshorn'

History: A modern shrub rose bred in Germany in 1951.

Description: A popular, large-growing shrub rose, 'Elmshorn' has very vigorous upright growth, reaches nearly 2 m (6½ ft) in height and spreads almost as wide when grown in the right situation. The foliage is dark green and glossy and makes a good backdrop for the flowers, which are produced in large trusses and are rounded in shape, creating a pompom-like effect. The flower colour is a rich and glowing deep pink, and the fragrance is most enjoyable.

Parentage: 'Hamburg' x 'Verdun'

Other names: None

Suggested usage: A wonderful large shrub, this rose makes an excellent background rose in a spacious border. It can also be grown as a large hedge, routinely trimmed back to maintain the shape. 'Elmshorn' is very adaptable, even in poorer soils.

'Eye Opener'

History: A Dutch-bred procumbent shrub rose, developed in 1987 and prized for its unusual blooms.

Description: This is a low-growing, spreading rose that only reaches 30 cm (1 ft) in height, but tends to spread to 1 m (3 ft) or more across the ground. The foliage is small and bright green in colour, with a healthy, glossy sheen. The flowers are the most brilliant red with white centres and prominent yellow stamens. This is a very interesting rose that is easy to grow in a wide range of soils.

Parentage: (seedling x 'Eyepaint') x (seedling x 'Dortmund')

Other names: 'Erica', 'Tapis Rouge'

Suggested usage: 'Eye Opener' is probably best grown as a groundcover, perhaps beneath a display of standard roses or combined with other red-flowering annuals and perennials. It can be grown in a container, where it will trail over the edge.

■ RECURRENT-FLOWERING
■ TOLERATES SOME SHADE
■ CAN BE CONTAINER-GROWN
■ DISEASE-RESISTANT

'Felicia'

History: An English-bred shrub rose, descended from the hybrid musk group, available since 1928.

Description: A handsome, bushy shrub, it grows to 1.2 m (4 ft), and has masses of glossy, mid-green foliage that provides a good backdrop for the flowers. The flowers are produced in large clusters, each being fully double in a warm shade of pink that can be a slightly deeper shade depending on the growing conditions. The flowers also have an appealing musky fragrance.

Parentage: 'Trier' x 'Ophelia'

Other names: None

Suggested usage: A very versatile and easy-to-grow rose in a wide range of conditions, it will tolerate poorer soils and even a little shade. This is a good all-rounder for beds, borders or containers.

■ RECURRENT-FLOWERING
■ TOLERATES SOME SHADE
■ CAN BE CONTAINER-GROWN
■ RELATIVELY DISEASE-FREE

'Fritz Nobis'

History: Bred in Germany in 1940, this rose is descended from a macrantha rose and carries some of its trailing characteristics.

Description: A very fine rose, 'Fritz Nobis' has been popular for decades, prized for its leathery, deep green foliage and arching growth habit. It can reach 1.2 m (4 ft) in height and spread if given plenty of space. The flowers are outstanding – large and well-formed, double blooms with delicate, soft pink petals that have ruffled edges, adding to the appeal. The blooms also have a sweet perfume and are excellent for cutting.

Parentage: 'Joanna Hill' x 'Magnifica'

Other names: None

Suggested usage: A hardy and adaptable rose, it is sometimes seen as a hedging plant, or trimmed hard as a rounded container specimen. Position it where the flowers can be easily appreciated.

▓ FLOWERS ONCE ONLY
▓ TOLERATES SOME SHADE
▓ CAN BE CONTAINER-GROWN
▓ RELATIVELY DISEASE-FREE

'Frühlingsgold'

History: A Scotch rose hybrid shrub, bred in Germany in 1937.

Description: A wonderful old shrub rose, this has remained popular since it was first introduced. Growing and spreading to more than 2 m (6½ ft), it has an upright, branching habit and masses of leathery, deep green foliage. The flowers are large and showy, opening from dainty yellow and red-tinged buds to produce open blooms with wonderful, clear primrose-yellow petals. It is extremely fragrant and, when in full bloom, fills the entire garden with sweet perfume.

Parentage: 'Joanna Hill' x R. pimpinellifolia hispida

Other names: 'Spring Gold'

Suggested usage: This is a rose that needs plenty of space to grow and spread. It is sometimes used as a background hedge, or planted against a wall or to disguise an unsightly building. It is very worthwhile.

▓ FLOWERS ONCE ONLY
▓ TOLERATES SOME SHADE
▓ RELATIVELY DISEASE-FREE

'Frühlingsmorgen'

History: A German-bred Scotch rose, first released in 1942 and prized for its outstanding flowers.

Description: A totally charming, large shrub rose, it grows and spreads to 1.5 m (5 ft) and has arching stems of mid-green foliage with a matt appearance. However, it is the flowers that really attract the eye, each one being large with creamy white petals that are brushed with a warm pink edging. The blooms also contain large yellow stamens that have a spidery effect in the centre, and they have a rich, sweet fragrance that adds to their charm.

Parentage: ('E. G. Hill' x 'Catherine' Kordes') x *R. pimpinellifolia altaica*

Other names: 'Spring Morning'

Suggested usage: This is a very good hedging rose, or background shrub for a mixed bed or border. It is easy-care and tolerant of poorer growing conditions.

■ FLOWERS ONCE ONLY
■ TOLERATES SOME SHADE
■ RELATIVELY DISEASE-FREE

'Golden Wings'

History: An excellent American-bred, modern shrub, released in 1956.

Description: For lovers of yellow roses, this one is exceptional. Growing to 1.5 m (5 ft) in height, and spreading almost as far, it has deep, rusty red stems and a good covering of light green, glossy foliage. The flowers are large and single, with clear yellow petals and rich golden-brown stamens that add greatly to the appeal of the blooms. It has a delicate fragrance and should flower all summer long if well cultivated.

Parentage: ('Soeur Thérèse' x *R. pimpinellifolia altaica*) x 'Ormiston Roy'

Other names: None

Suggested usage: A very worthwhile hedging shrub, it will adapt to a wide range of soils and climates. It is wonderful in a hot-colour flower bed of yellows, oranges and splashes of red.

- ▓ RECURRENT-FLOWERING
- ▓ TOLERATES SOME SHADE
- ▓ RELATIVELY DISEASE-FREE

'James Mason'

History: Bred in Britain in 1982, a gallica-style modern shrub with outstandingly rich crimson flowers.

Description: One of the best crimson-flowering shrub roses, it grows to 1.4 m (4½ ft) and also spreads quite widely. It has mid-green, matt foliage that acts as a good foil for the showy flowers. Each bloom is large and almost single, with papery, crimson petals and prominent yellow stamens. The flowers are prolific, even if the flowering time is relatively short. They are also very fragrant, which adds to their appeal.

Parentage: 'Scharlachglut' x 'Tuscany Superb'

Other names: None

Suggested usage: This is a good rose to plant in a bed where crimson is needed – perhaps as a vivid contrast to blue- and purple-flowering annuals and perennials. It is also fantastic for a container, and is hardy and easy to cultivate.

- ▓ FLOWERS ONCE ONLY
- ▓ FULL SUN
- ▓ CAN BE CONTAINER-GROWN
- ▓ RELATIVELY DISEASE-FREE

'Nevada'

History: An old shrub rose bred in Spain in 1927, but still widely cultivated to this day.

Description: A very popular old shrub rose, it is prized for its showy and prolific blooms. Growing to 2.5 m (8 ft) and spreading almost as far, it is a vigorous shrub with a dense growth of stems that are covered with deep green, semi-glossy foliage. The flowers are very large and open, with creamy yellow flowers that are flushed with pink, fading to white as they age. The flowers have prominent golden stamens which are also very showy, and they produce a light, wafting fragrance.

Parentage: Slightly obscure. Could be a hybrid of *R. moyesii* or *R. pimpinellifolia*

Other names: None

Suggested usage: This shrubs needs lots of space to grow and spread, and is ideal for the back of a deep flower border or as a tall hedge against a fence or wall.

- RECURRENT-FLOWERING
- FULL SUN
- RELATIVELY DISEASE-FREE

'Penelope'

History: An old English-bred shrub rose, released in 1924 and based on hybrid musk lineage.

Description: Still a popular old shrub rose, it grows to 1.2 m (4 ft), and has a compact, rounded shape and masses of deep green foliage that is glossy and healthy throughout the season. The flowers are produced in large clusters, each bloom being semi-double with creamy petals flushed with pink. 'Penelope' is very free-flowering and is also fragrant. The spent flowerheads produce ornamental hips in the autumn.

Parentage: 'Ophelia' x seedling

Other names: None

Suggested usage: A versatile rose, 'Penelope' is prized for its ability to tolerate poorer growing conditions. It is sometimes grown as a hedge, or as a container plant. It is prone to mildew if overcrowded.

- RECURRENT-FLOWERING
- FULL SUN
- CAN BE CONTAINER-GROWN
- RELATIVELY DISEASE-FREE

'Scarlet Fire'

History: An old gallica hybrid shrub rose, bred in Germany in 1952.

Description: A very large and vigorous shrub, it can reach 3 m (10 ft) or more and spread almost as wide if allowed space to develop. The foliage is glossy with a bronzy tinge, and is carried on virtually thornless, brown-purple stems. The flowers are large, showy and single with brilliant red petals and glossy yellow stamens. The flowers are followed by decorative, urn-shaped, orange hips in the autumn.

Parentage: 'Poinsettia' x 'Alika'

Other names: 'Scarlet Glow', 'Scharlachglut'

Suggested usage: For large gardens with deep flower borders, this rose is outstanding. It needs plenty of space, although of course it can be pruned back hard to keep it more compact.

▓ FLOWERS ONCE ONLY
▓ FULL SUN
▓ RELATIVELY DISEASE-FREE

'Zigeunerknabe'

History: An old shrub rose, sometimes classified as a hybrid bourbon rose, developed in Germany in 1909.

Description: A compact, rounded shrub, it grows to 1.5 m (5 ft) in height, and has thick, leathery leaves that are quite heavily veined. The flowers are outstanding – medium-sized and fully double, with rich crimson petals and primrose-yellow stamens that produce a brilliant contrast. The flowers tend to fade in the hot summer sun, so a little shade is preferable.

Parentage: 'Russelliana' x *R. rugosa* seedling

Other names: 'Gipsy Boy'

Suggested usage: This is a good, medium-sized shrub rose for borders, positioned where some shade can be provided in the middle of the day. It can also be grown against a short trellis, or in a pot.

▓ RECURRENT-FLOWERING
▓ TOLERATES SOME SHADE
▓ CAN BE CONTAINER-GROWN
▓ RELATIVELY DISEASE-FREE

CLIMBING AND RAMBLING
ROSES

Roses that develop long, pliable stems that can be trained to cover walls and archways are generally defined as 'climbers'; while those that also have a large growth habit but a more bushy appearance are known as 'ramblers'. The main difference in the cultivation of these two types is the pruning – climbers can be controlled with routine cutting of side shoots to encourage flowering, while ramblers tend to have a mind of their own and can only be pruned in a rough, rather haphazard fashion to keep them under control. Ideally they should just be allowed to develop their own shape, and therefore they need space to grow – larger country gardens are ideal for this purpose.

Caution must be exercised when planting either climbers or ramblers. For example, a rampant climber with nasty thorns shouldn't be planted on an archway where people will be walking. Likewise, a rambler that will rapidly triple in size and overwhelm nearby plants should be avoided in smaller gardens.

PREVIOUS PAGE Cherokee rose

'Albéric Barbier'

History: Bred in France in 1900, this is another excellent climber based on the wichuraiana rambler.

Description: A charming, old-world climber, this rose has the most wonderfully fragrant flowers. It is vigorous and tall-growing, capable of reaching 6 m (20 ft) or more, and has long, pliable stems and masses of rich, deep green, glossy foliage. The flowers begin as dainty yellow buds, opening to large, double or semi-double blooms with soft creamy white petals. This rose is also virtually thornless, which is a bonus for many gardeners.

Parentage: *R. wichuraiana* x 'Shirley Hibberd'

Other names: None

Suggested usage: 'Albéric Barbier' is easy to train over an archway or trellis because of its thornless, pliable stems. It makes a wonderful display in full flush, then spot-flowers again later in the season.

■ RECURRENT-FLOWERING
■ TOLERATES SOME SHADE
■ RELATIVELY DISEASE-FREE

'Albertine'

History: An charming old-fashioned climber, bred from a wichuraiana rambler in France in 1921, and still extremely popular.

Description: This is a vigorous and very thorny rose that can reach 6 m (20 ft) or more, with thick, stiff stems and masses of glossy, deep green foliage that at times has a burnished red appearance. The flowers are divine – opening from neat pink buds to large, muddled flowers with coppery pink petals with a touch of gold in the throat. The flowers are prolific when in bloom, and also highly fragrant. This is a favourite with many gardeners.

Parentage: *R. wichuraiana* x 'Mrs. A. R. Waddell'

Other names: None

Suggested usage: 'Albertine' is not a climber for an archway or gate because the hooked thorns can be quite vicious. Train it against a trellis or over a wall – the stems are stiff and need to be worked into position while still pliable.

■ FLOWERS ONCE ONLY
■ TOLERATES SOME SHADE
■ RELATIVELY DISEASE-FREE

■ RECURRENT-FLOWERING
░ FULL SUN
░ CAN BE CONTAINER-GROWN
■ RELATIVELY DISEASE-FREE

'Aloha'

History: A modern, large-flowered climber bred in the United States in 1949.

Description: 'Aloha' is a very versatile and easy-to-grow climber that reaches 3 m (10 ft) in height, with upright stems and masses of glossy, deep green leaves touched with bronze. The flowers are very large and shapely and produced in profusion for a long period. The blooms are rounded and fully double with rose-pink petals that have a deeper reverse, and hints of magenta and salmon pink in the centre. This is a truly outstanding variety of rose.

Parentage: 'Mercedes Gallart' x 'New Dawn'

Other names: None

Suggested usage: 'Aloha' is suitable for training against a fence or wall, or growing over an archway or trellis. It is quite slow-growing but easy to train.

'Altissimo'

History: A modern, cluster-flowered climber, bred in France in 1966 and still considered one of the best red-flowering climbers on the market.

Description: This is a really outstanding floribunda climber that reaches 3.5 m (11½ ft) in height, with angular, upright growth and a good covering of glossy, deep green foliage. The flowers are produced in clusters and are very large and single with bright red petals and prominent yellow stamens that are also very showy. The effect in full flower is spectacular and the flowers are long-lasting, hold their colour well and also have a slight fragrance.

Parentage: 'Tenor' x unknown seedling

Other names: None

Suggested usage: An easy-to-grow climber for most situations, it needs to be trained as the young pliable stems are produced, taking care of the thorns. It can also be kept pruned back as a tall shrub.

■ RECURRENT-FLOWERING
▨ FULL SUN
■ RELATIVELY DISEASE-FREE

'American Pillar'

History: A famous and popular climber, bred by van Fleet in the United States in 1902 from a local wild rose mingled with a wichuraiana rambler.

Description: This is an outstanding climber for its multitude of slender, upright stems that can be trained to form a spectacular column of flowers. Growing to 5 m (16½ ft) or more, it is very robust with deep green, glossy foliage and small, reddish pink flowers with a white centre that smother the stems for several weeks in summer. Rain will spoil the flowers and also tends to cause mildew, so choose a sunny, open spot.

Parentage: (*R. wichuraiana* x *R. setigera*) x 'Red Letter Day'

Other names: None

Suggested usage: 'American Pillar' is a wonderful rose to train up a veranda post or pillar, or to weave through a chain to form a 'swag'. It is also suitable for growing up into trees.

■ FLOWERS ONCE ONLY
■ FULL SUN
■ SUSCEPTIBLE TO BLACK SPOT

'Belle Portugaise'

History: Bred in Portugal in 1900, this outstanding climber is a descendant of a gigantea climber from the Himalayas which, in turn, is also a parent plant to the old-fashioned tea roses.

Description: A very large and vigorous climber, this grows to 6 m (20 ft) or more, and has deep green, ruffled foliage and lots of pliable, upward stems. The flowers are prolific in summer – large and semi-double with loose petals of pale pink with slightly deeper pink shadings. Although it flowers only once, it does so for quite a long period and is very showy.

Parentage: *R. gigantea* x 'Reine Marie Henriette'

Other names: 'Belle of Portugal'

Suggested usage: This is a good, all-purpose climber for covering walls, fences or outbuildings, or to allow to clamber into trees. A warm, sheltered position is best, as this rose doesn't like too much cold weather.

■ FLOWERS ONLY ONCE
■ FULL SUN
■ RELATIVELY DISEASE-FREE

'Blairii Number Two'

History: A very old bourbon climber, dating back to 1845 and bred in Britain.

Description: A lovely old-fashioned climber, this rose is vigorous and thorny, and grows to 4 m (13 ft). It has a good covering of mid-green foliage that is wonderfully tinted with burgundy when young. The flowers are prolific – large and flat with pale pink petals that are a deeper shade of pink towards the centre. The flowers are delightfully fragrant and, although this rose blooms only once during the season, it does so for a very long period, making it more than worthwhile.

Parentage: Unknown

Other names: None

Suggested usage: This is an excellent rose to train onto a pillar or tripod because of the density of the flowers. It tends to succumb to mildew late in the season, so make sure the area around the plant is weed-free and well ventilated.

■ FLOWERS ONCE ONLY
■ FULL SUN
■ RELATIVELY DISEASE-FREE

'Bloomfield Courage'

History: A rather obscure cluster-flowered climber first noted in the United States in 1925.

Description: A vigorous, upright climber, reaching a height of 4.5 m (15 ft), it has a multitude of strong stems and a good covering of attractive, glossy green foliage. The flowers are quite small but prolific, and carried in clusters. Tight red buds open to virtually single, velvety red flowers with white centres and prominent yellow stamens. This rose is a knockout when in full bloom.

Parentage: Unknown

Other names: None

Suggested usage: 'Bloomfield Courage' is a good rose to allow to clamber up into trees or to smother a fence or old shed. It doesn't do well in very cold climates, preferring a warm, sheltered situation.

■ FLOWERS ONCE ONLY
■ FULL SUN
■ RELATIVELY DISEASE-FREE

'Clair Matin'

History: This is a climbing sport of the famous floribunda of the same name, and was introduced in France in 1963.

Description: An elegant, arching climber, it has stems to 2.2 m (7¼ ft) in length and masses of deep green, glossy foliage. When the rose is in full bloom, the stems can be dragged down with the sheer weight of the clusters, so good support is essential. The flowers are medium-sized, with beautiful petals of pale pink with deeper pink or bronze highlights. The effect is very showy during the summer as the flowers continue to appear right through the season.

Parentage: 'Fashion' x [('Independence' x 'Orange Triumph') x 'Phyllis Bide']

Other names: 'Meimont'

Suggested usage: This is a good, all-purpose climber for archways, trellises or tripods. Keep deadheading the spent flower clusters and it will reward with new growth.

- RECURRENT-FLOWERING
- FULL SUN
- CAN BE CONTAINER-GROWN
- RELATIVELY DISEASE-FREE

'Compassion'

History: A modern, climbing hybrid tea rose developed in Britain in 1973.

Description: A vigorous upright climber, 'Compassion' grows to 3 m (10 ft), and has stiff, angular stems and dark, very glossy foliage that remains healthy and lush right through the season. The flowers are carried on strong stems, each bloom being shapely and high-centred with apricot-copper petals that have cream and yellow highlights. This rose also features a very pleasant fragrance and is suitable for cutting.

Parentage: 'White Cocktail' x 'Prima Ballerina'

Other names: 'Belle de Londres'

Suggested usage: 'Compassion' is an easy-care rose that can be grown in a wide range of soils and climates. Start training the shoots as they grow, weaving them over archways or through trellis – or just allow it to clamber over a fence or wall.

RECURRENT-FLOWERING
FULL SUN
DISEASE-RESISTANT

FLOWERS ONCE ONLY
TOLERATES SOME SHADE
RELATIVELY DISEASE-FREE

'Constance Spry'

History: An all-time favourite shrubby climber, released by David Austin in Britain in 1961, and remaining popular with gardeners everywhere ever since.

Description: This climber has the gentle looks of an old-fashioned rose with all the benefits of modern hybrids – prolific flowering and relatively good disease-resistance. Growing to 6 m (20 ft) or more, it has coarse, leathery, mid-green foliage and wonderful, large, fully double flowers that are rich pink with a strong, myrrh-like fragrance. Its sheer size is daunting in smaller gardens, unless it is pruned back hard to keep it under control.

Parentage: 'Belle Isis' x 'Dainty Maid'

Other names: None

Suggested usage: This rose can be allowed to grow wild over fences and walls, or trained more formally to cover a large archway. When it is in full bloom the impact of this rose is spectacular.

'Dublin Bay'

History: An outstanding cluster-flowered climber bred by the expatriate Irish breeder McGredy in New Zealand in 1976.

Description: A very rewarding red-flowered climber, it grows to 2 m (6½ ft) or more, and has masses of healthy, bright green foliage right through the season. The flowers, which stand out brilliantly from the foliage, are carried in showy clusters, each bloom being medium-sized in a rich blood red. The flowers have a slight fragrance and are good for cutting, which in turn encourages even more flowering.

Parentage: 'Bantry Bay' x 'Altissimo'

Other names: 'Macdub'

Suggested usage: This is a compact climber for smaller gardens, prized for its health and gorgeous flowers. Train it onto a pillar or tripod for an outstanding effect.

- RECURRENT-FLOWERING
- FULL SUN
- CAN BE CONTAINER-GROWN
- DISEASE-RESISTANT

'Félicité et Perpétue'

History: An old-fashioned rambler developed in France in 1827 by the head gardener to the Duke of Orleans.

Description: A vigorous, old rambling rose, it reaches more than 6 m (20 ft) in height if left unpruned. It has relatively thornless stems and healthy, mid-green foliage that is glossy and attractive even when the rose is not in flower. The blooms are small but prolific, opening from tight, reddish pink buds to fully double, creamy white flowers that are richly scented – adding to its appeal.

Parentage: Unknown

Other names: None

Suggested usage: A good rose for an old-fashioned or cottage garden; leave it to ramble over a fence or wall or train it against a trellis or archway. Nip off the spent blooms to keep it looking tidy.

▓ FLOWERS ONCE ONLY
▓ FULL SUN
▓ RELATIVELY DISEASE-FREE

'Golden Showers'

History: A popular modern floribunda climber bred in the United States in 1957 and still widely cultivated in domestic gardens.

Description: When seen in full flower the popularity of this climber is easily understood. Growing to 3.5 m (11½ ft) or more, it makes strong, spreading growth with very healthy, mid-green foliage. The flowers are produced in large, rather loose clusters, each bloom being rounded, with ruffled petals in the most glorious shade of deep golden-yellow. The flowers are also slightly fragrant and last for a long time before fading.

Parentage: 'Charlotte Armstrong' x 'Captain Thomas'

Other names: None

Suggested usage: This is a wonderful all-round rose for archways or to train against a wall for a dramatic effect. It can also be kept pruned back hard as a large, generous shrub.

▓ RECURRENT-FLOWERING
▓ FULL SUN
▓ RELATIVELY DISEASE-FREE

'Goldfinch'

History: A charming, old-world polyantha climber raised by the English breeder Paul in 1907.

Description: This absolutely delightful old rambler grows to 2 m (6½ ft) in height, and has bushy, upright, thornless stems and masses of mid-green, glossy foliage. The flowers are small but prolific, opening from tight yellow buds to produce cup-shaped, semi-double flowers that are golden-yellow fading to cream. The overall effect in flowering with various yellows and creams on the same bush is most attractive.

Parentage: 'Helene' x ('Aglaia' x 'Crimson Rambler')

Other names: None

Suggested usage: This is a perfect rose for a country garden, where it can be used as an informal hedge or just allowed to grow wild. It is very easy to cultivate.

▉ FLOWERS ONCE ONLY
▉ TOLERATES SOME SHADE
▉ RELATIVELY DISEASE-FREE

'Guinée'

History: A worthwhile, old climbing tea rose developed in France in 1938 and still prized for its velvety blooms.

Description: A very vigorous upright climber, it can reach 6 m (20 ft) or more if allowed to have its way. The growth is sturdy and angular, with plenty of leathery, deep green foliage that is semi-glossy and generally very healthy. The flowers are spectacular – large and fully-double with rich crimson petals that are velvety. As the rose opens it has a muddled appearance, revealing the bright yellow stamens in the centre. It is very fragrant and prolific, and a hard rose to surpass.

Parentage: 'Souvenir de Claudius Denoyel' x 'Ami Quinard'

Other names: None

Suggested usage: Allow this rose to clamber over fences and walls, or train it against a trellis for a fantastic summer display. It will repeat-flower, but not as prolifically.

▉ RECURRENT-FLOWERING
▉ FULL SUN
▉ RELATIVELY DISEASE-FREE

'Joseph's Coat'

History: A modern floribunda climber developed in the United States in 1964 and valued for its multicoloured flowers.

Description: A vigorous, tall floribunda, this rose can be grown either as a shrub or a climber, depending on its position. Its natural height is about 2.5 m (8 ft), and it has strong, upright stems and plenty of glossy, light green foliage. The dramatic flowers are carried in showy clusters and are semi-double with petals in various shades of oranges and yellows. Although the flowers are not scented, this is a good rose for cutting because of the unusual colouring.

Parentage: 'Buccaneer' x 'Circus'

Other names: None

Suggested usage: A rose to feature prominently if you like bright colours in the garden, it can be trained around a pillar or tripod, or against a wall. Deadhead regularly to encourage more flowers.

- RECURRENT-FLOWERING
- FULL SUN
- RELATIVELY DISEASE-FREE

'Maigold'

History: A popular cluster-flowered climber developed by Kordes in Germany in 1953 and still widely cultivated.

Description: Although this climber only flowers during the summer, the display is long lived and spectacular, making it a most worthwhile plant. Growing to 3.5 m (11½ ft) in height, it produces strong, prickly stems with red thorns and plenty of mid-green, glossy foliage. The flowers are carried in large clusters and are semi-double with golden-yellow petals that are lightly flushed with orange. It has an excellent scent.

Parentage: 'Poulson's Pink' x 'Frühlingstag'

Other names: None

Suggested usage: This is a wonderful rose to grow against a sunny wall or fence, or over a large archway that can carry the weight. Regular removal of the spent flowers encourages more flowering.

FLOWERS ONCE ONLY
FULL SUN
RELATIVELY DISEASE-FREE

'Meg'

History: An unusual floribunda climber introduced into Britain in 1954.

Description: A vigorous, upright floribunda climber, this rose can reach 4 m (13 ft) in height in the right situation. The foliage is mid-green and semi-glossy and the flowers are large and semi-double with unusual, soft bronze-apricot petals that fade to cream with age. The stamens are golden-yellow and prominent and the rose has a light, but appealing fragrance.

Parentage: 'Paul's Lemon Pillar' x 'Mme Butterfly'

Other names: None

Suggested usage: Position this rose against a wall, or allow it simply to ramble. It can also be grown up into trees to great effect.

■ RECURRENT-FLOWERING
▨ FULL SUN
■ RELATIVELY DISEASE-FREE

'Mermaid'

History: One of the best-loved old climbers, bred from a wild rose by the English breeder Paul in 1918.

Description: A magnificent, rampant climber, this is best suited to large gardens where it can be allowed to go wild. Growing to 10 m (33 ft) or more, it forms a huge mass of thorny brown stems smothered in glossy green foliage. The huge, single flowers appear continuously through the summer. They are up to 15 cm (6 in) across, with pale yellow petals and rich amber-yellow stamens. This is one of the best yellow climbers.

Parentage: *R. bracteata* x double yellow tea rose

Other names: *R. bracteata*

Suggested usage: 'Mermaid' is a wonderful plant to create an impenetrable hedge, left entirely unpruned. It can also be grown with more control, cut back regularly and trained against a wall. However, the thorns are to be avoided.

■ RECURRENT-FLOWERING
▨ FULL SUN
■ RELATIVELY DISEASE-FREE

'Mme Grégoire Staechelin'

History: A wonderful, old, large-flowered climber bred in Spain in 1927 and still admired for its large, soft blooms.

Description: A vigorous and quickly spreading climber, this rose can reach 5 m (16½ ft) in height, and has masses of deep green foliage with a matt finish. The flowers are very large and open and almost double, with ruffled, pale pink petals that are edged and reversed in a deep shade of pink. The flowers are also highly fragrant and followed by showy, urn-shaped hips in autumn.

Parentage: 'Frau Karl Druschki' x 'Château de Clos Vougeot'

Other names: 'Spanish Beauty'

Suggested usage: A very reliable climber for difficult situations, this rose tolerates poor soils and shade. Plant it against a wall or fence and allow it to remain unpruned and undeadheaded to enjoy the autumn hips.

FLOWERS ONCE ONLY
TOLERATES SOME SHADE
RELATIVELY DISEASE-FREE

'Nancy Hayward'

History: A modern, large-flowered climber bred in Australia in 1937. It is sometimes difficult to obtain, but worth searching out for the collector.

Description: An outstanding climber, 'Nancy Hayward' is prized for the unusual colour of the flowers. Growing to only 2 m (6½ ft) in height, it is a robust, healthy plant with lots of lush, green foliage and large, open, single flowers in a rich shade of tomato-red. The petals are very delicate and papery, and the stamens in the centre are also most appealing. This rose thrives in warm to hot climates.

Parentage: 'Jessie Clark' x unknown seedling

Other names: None

Suggested usage: Plant this rose against a warm, sunny wall or fence and train it through wire or trellis. It can also be pruned back and grown as a tall shrub. It is most rewarding if well tended.

▧ RECURRENT-FLOWERING
▨ FULL SUN
▧ RELATIVELY DISEASE-FREE

'New Dawn'

History: One of the most popular and widely grown pink climbers, bred in the United States in 1930 from a wichuraiana rambler.

Description: A very vigorous, healthy and fast-growing climber, 'New Dawn' has a plentiful supply of grey-green, semi-glossy foliage that remains healthy right through the season. The flowers open from plump, deep pink buds to semi-double blooms with soft, silvery pink petals and golden stamens. The flowers are sweetly fragrant, which adds to this rose's charm. This is an outstanding variety.

Parentage: Sport of 'Dr W. van Fleet'

Other names: None

Suggested usage: 'New Dawn' is a very versatile rose that is easy to cultivate even in poor growing conditions. Plant it against a wall, or train it over an archway, for a long-lasting display.

▧ RECURRENT-FLOWERING
▨ TOLERATES SOME SHADE
▧ RELATIVELY DISEASE-FREE

'Paradise'

History: A cluster-flowered, modern climber bred in the United States in 1953, often grown in display gardens.

Description: 'Paradise' is a rather lovely climber that can grow to 3 m (10 ft) in height or be kept more compact with routine pruning. It has healthy, deep green foliage that is glossy and plentiful, as well as very beautiful cerise to crimson, fully double flowers that have a shimmering appearance like Thai silk. The flowers are highly fragrant and prolific in the summer and are also excellent for cutting.

Parentage: 'New Dawn' seedling x 'World's Fair'

Other names: None

Suggested usage: This is an outstanding rose for training up a pillar or veranda post, to create a column of shimmering colour that will last for several months.

■ RECURRENT-FLOWERING
▨ FULL SUN
■ RELATIVELY DISEASE-FREE

'Paul's Lemon Pillar'

History: An old-fashioned, climbing, hybrid tea rose developed in Britain is 1915.

Description: A sturdy, upright climber that reaches 4 m (13 ft) in height, it develops many branches that are covered with sharp thorns. The foliage is large and a soft grey-green in colour, setting off the beauty of the flowers. Each bloom is large and shapely, with creamy white petals tinged with lemon-yellow. The flowers are richly scented and also prized for their ability to withstand rainfall.

Parentage: 'Frau Karl Druschki' x 'Maréchal Niel'

Other names: None

Suggested usage: 'Paul's Lemon Pillar' is a good rose for winding around an upright pillar or post, to create a long floral display in summer.

■ FLOWERS ONCE ONLY
▨ FULL SUN
■ RELATIVELY DISEASE-FREE

'Paul's Scarlet Climber'

History: A very famous old polyantha climber, developed by the English breeder Paul in 1916 and still commonly grown to this day.

Description: A wonderful old climber with upright stems, this rose reaches 3 m (10 ft) in height, and has deep green, matt foliage. The flowers are prolific and carried in clusters, each bloom being medium-sized, semi-double and a rich scarlet-red. The flowers hold their shape and colour well for long periods. This is a delightful variety.

Parentage: 'Paul's Carmine Pillar' x 'Rêve d'Or'

Other names: 'Paul's Scarlet'

Suggested usage: This is a very easy-care climber for difficult growing conditions. It can be trained over an archway as it has very few thorns, or against a sunny wall.

- FLOWERS ONCE ONLY
- TOLERATES SOME SHADE
- RELATIVELY DISEASE-FREE

'Sander's White'

History: A lovely old wichuraiana rambler bred in Britain in 1912.

Description: A vigorous, old-fashioned rambling rose, it can grow to 3.5 m (11½ ft) and has a relaxed, bushy habit and masses of mid-green, semi-glossy foliage right through the season. The small, white, rosette-shaped flowers open from tight pink buds and are highly fragrant. The blooms are generally carried in cascading clusters which are most attractive.

Parentage: Unknown

Other names: None

Suggested usage: 'Sander's White' is a wonderful rose for an old-fashioned or cottage garden, if there is space to let it ramble. It can be trained into a weeping standard or allowed to clamber into deciduous trees.

▪ FLOWERS ONCE ONLY
▪ TOLERATES SOME SHADE
▪ RELATIVELY DISEASE-FREE

'Veilchenblau'

History: A very pretty old polyantha climber bred in Germany in 1909 and still highly prized.

Description: A bushy, branching rambler, it can reach 4 m (13 ft) in height, and has masses of thornless stems and glossy, mid-green foliage. The flowers are small and produced in large, showy trusses. Each bloom is semi-double, with delicate, lavender-purple petals – sometimes flecked with white – with prominent yellow stamens. This is a very worthwhile rambler.

Parentage: 'Crimson Rambler' x 'Erinnerung an Brod'

Other names: 'Blue Rambler', 'Blue Rosalie', 'Violet Blue'

Suggested usage: Allow this rose to grow wild over fences, or up into trees, for a wonderful summer display of flowers. It can also be pruned into a more controlled shape if desired.

▓ FLOWERS ONCE ONLY
▓ TOLERATES SOME SHADE
▓ RELATIVELY DISEASE-FREE

'Wedding Day'

History: A very old rose, presumed to be an accidental cross with a sinowilsonii rambler, discovered in Britain in 1950.

Description: A very large-growing and vigorous rose, it can reach 9 m (29½ ft) or more if left unpruned, and has a good covering of bright green, glossy foliage which acts as a perfect backdrop for the flowers. The flowers are carried in large clusters or trusses – each bloom is small, single and white with very showy orange stamens in the centre. The flowers are highly fragrant and prized for bridal bouquets.

Parentage: *R. sinowilsonii* x unknown seedling

Other names: None

Suggested usage: A very fast-growing and easy-care rose, it can be allowed to ramble across the ground as a groundcover, or to shoot up into trees. It will tolerate poor growing conditions and semi-shade.

▓ FLOWERS ONCE ONLY
▓ TOLERATES SOME SHADE
▓ RELATIVELY DISEASE-FREE

MINIATURE AND DWARF
ROSES

Also commonly known as patio roses, these compact and delightful plants were first bred commercially in the 1920s, and have been popular with gardeners and florists ever since. The first true miniature rose was introduced into cultivation in Switzerland in 1922 and named 'Roulettii', after Dr Roulet who discovered it growing as a potted plant in a small Swiss village. It was identified as a mutated form of *Rosa chinensis* 'Pumila', and it was the first recognized rose plant to combine miniature size with showy blooms. 'Roulettii' is now the parent of many of the modern, cultivated miniature and dwarf roses which have been bred in the most amazing range of colours and flower forms – from simple, single blooms ('Robin Red Breast') to complex, fully double forms ('Amy Brown'), in colours ranging from pure white, through every shade of pink and red, to orange and yellow.

Included in this group are the dwarf polyantha roses, a fascinating small group of roses believed to have evolved from an accidental cross between *R. multiflora* and *R. chinensis*. They are charming, small-growing roses with flowers that are highly prized by florists, and which make charming potted roses for summer display.

PREVIOUS PAGE 'Baby Masquerade'

'Ballerina'

History: A charming old polyantha rose, dating back to 1937, which has been a favourite with florists since that time.

Description: A spreading, open shrub, 'Ballerina' grows to to 1 m (3 ft), and has masses of semi-glossy, mid-green foliage. The flowers are prolific right through the season, appearing as large sprays of small, dainty, light pink blooms that are followed by small orange hips that are also highly decorative. The blooms from this rose are often cut and used for floral arrangements. 'Ballerina' can either be pruned regularly to keep a compact shape, or allowed to develop its own natural, appealing habit.

Parentage: Unknown

Other names: None

Suggested usage: Plant this rose in a large tub and position it in a prominent place during summer. 'Ballerina' is also often grown as a compact floral hedge.

■ RECURRENT-FLOWERING
■ TOLERATES SOME SHADE
■ CAN BE CONTAINER-GROWN
■ RELATIVELY DISEASE-FREE

'Bassino'

History: A modern, groundcovering rose developed by the German rose breeders Kordes in 1988.

Description: This is a useful, small-growing rose that is prized for its rapid growth and healthy, disease-free foliage. Growing to 60 cm (2 ft) at most, it has a sprawling habit and masses of deep green, glossy foliage with dramatic, deep scarlet flowers that feature prominent yellow stamens – the effect being of a yellow 'eye'. The flowers are lightly fragrant and, if grown well, will be prolific for many months in the summer.

Parentage: Unknown

Other names: None

Suggested usage: Like most groundcovering roses, 'Bassino' is an excellent plant for the front of a mixed border, where it can be trimmed to prevent it from taking over the garden bed. It is most dramatic when mass-planted and should provide a good display for lengthy periods.

■ RECURRENT-FLOWERING
■ FULL SUN
■ DISEASE-RESISTANT

'China Doll'

History: An American-bred rose, classified as a dwarf polyantha, introduced to gardens in 1946.

Description: A charming old border rose, this grows to only 50 cm (1¾ ft) in height, and has masses of healthy, light green foliage that forms a perfect backdrop to the flowers. The blooms are carried in large, showy trusses, each one quite large and cup-shaped with marvellous China-pink, ruffled petals. This is an easy-to-grow, reliable, small rose for a wide range of soils and climates.

Parentage: 'Mrs Dudley Fulton' x 'Tom Thumb'

Other names: None

Suggested usage: Frequently seen as a border or hedging rose, it can be kept tidy by routine deadheading. It will flower prolifically in a container, producing colour right through the season.

- RECURRENT-FLOWERING
- FULL SUN
- CAN BE CONTAINER-GROWN
- DISEASE-RESISTANT

'Cinderella'

History: Bred in Holland in 1953, this charming miniature has long been a favourite among gardeners.

Description: A wonderful small rose, 'Cinderella' is ideal for container cultivation because of its compact size. Growing and spreading to no more than 30 cm (1 ft), it forms a dense, upright mass of thornless stems that are well clothed in light green foliage. The flowers are prolific, slightly double and rather fluffy in appearance, with whitish petals that are tinged with pink. This is a very worthwhile and adaptable rose.

Parentage: 'Cécile Brunner' x 'Peon'

Other names: None

Suggested usage: A perfect container rose, it can be mass-planted in a window box to great effect, or used simply as a single pot plant placed prominently where its flowers can be enjoyed in summer.

- RECURRENT-FLOWERING
- FULL SUN
- CAN BE CONTAINER-GROWN
- RELATIVELY DISEASE-FREE

'Claret Cup'

History: A hardy, low-growing rose produced in the United States in 1976 by breeder Griffith Buck.

Description: An old-fashioned looking rose, 'Claret Cup' can grow to 1.2 m (4 ft) if left unpruned, and has a good covering of deep green, disease-resistant foliage and showy clusters of cup-shaped, light claret-coloured blooms that have a pale flush from the base. The petals sometimes feature a scattering of freckles, which adds to their appeal. The flowers are fragrant and followed by attractive bright red hips in the autumn.

Parentage: Unknown

Other names: 'Sevilliana'

Suggested usage: A perfect rose for cool to cold climates, it can be grown in a container in a sunny situation, or as part of a mixed border with other plants in the red, yellow and orange colour range. It can be pruned hard to maintain low growth.

■ RECURRENT-FLOWERING
■ TOLERATES SOME SHADE
■ CAN BE CONTAINER-GROWN
■ DISEASE-RESISTANT

'Magic Carousel'

History: A delightful, pink-flowering miniature rose bred in the United States in 1972.

Description: A small, well-shaped bush, it grows to 40 cm (1¼ ft) in height, and has a good covering of small, clear green leaves which are glossy and remain healthy right through the season. The flowers are multipetalled and carried in clusters, forming a compact rosette shape with petals that are cream to yellow, deeply edged in pink. The blooms have a delicate perfume and are perfect for cutting and use in dainty floral arrangements.

Parentage: 'Little Darling' x 'Westmont'

Other names: 'Morrousel'

Suggested usage: The health and vigour of this rose make it ideal for home gardeners. It is a perfect container plant for either full sun or semi-shaded spots.

■ RECURRENT-FLOWERING
■ TOLERATES SOME SHADE
■ CAN BE CONTAINER-GROWN
■ DISEASE-RESISTANT

'Orange Sunblaze'

History: A strongly colourful, miniature floribunda bred by Meilland in France and introduced to gardens in 1982. There is also a climbing variety of this rose.

Description: A dainty, small bush, growing no more than 30 cm (1 ft) in height, it has masses of small, pointed, pale green leaves that make an attractive backdrop to the flowers. From late spring onwards the entire bush is covered with clusters of small, rosette-shaped flowers in brilliant orange-red – they are delightfully fragrant and are ideal for cutting or exhibition. This is a very vibrant plant.

Parentage: 'Parador' x ('Baby Bettina' x 'Duchess of Windsor')

Other names: 'Orange Meillandina', 'Sunblaze'

Suggested usage: This rose is made for mass-planting across a sunny bed where the rich blooms will look very dramatic. It is also an excellent container plant, positioned in a sunny, prominent place when in bloom.

- RECURRENT-FLOWERING
- FULL SUN
- CAN BE CONTAINER-GROWN
- RELATIVELY DISEASE-FREE

'Pride 'n' Joy'

History: An award-winning miniature bred in the United States and introduced in 1991.

Description: A vigorous, bushy rose, this is slightly larger than most miniatures, growing to 60 cm (2 ft) high, with plenty of glossy, deep green foliage that remains healthy on the plant right through the season. The flowers are outstanding and are carried on tall, strong stems. Each bloom opens from a soft orange bud to a high-centred, double rose in various shades of tangerine, copper and pink. The overall effect of the bush, when in full flower, is spectacular.

Parentage: 'Chattem Centennial' x 'Prominent'

Other names: 'Jacmo'

Suggested usage: This is another perfect miniature for a container, or for mass-planting in a sunny, open bed. It combines well with other warm flower tones of yellow, cream and apricot.

■ RECURRENT-FLOWERING
▨ FULL SUN
■ CAN BE CONTAINER-GROWN
■ RELATIVELY DISEASE-FREE

'Rainbow's End'

History: An American-bred miniature introduced in 1984, still popular for cutting and exhibition.

Description: An outstanding miniature for the perfect shape and colour of its flowers, it grows to 40 cm (15¾ in), and has masses of small, pointed, light green leaves. It has strong stems with quite prominent thorns, which makes deadheading a bit of a challenge. The flowers are high-centred, classic, tiny and hybrid tea-shaped, with petals of rich yellow edged in deep pinky red. Both buds and flowers are ideal for cutting.

Parentage: Not known

Other names: 'Savalife'

Suggested usage: A wonderful specimen rose for a container, it will attract attention right through the season. It could also be used as a low hedge or border to great effect.

■ RECURRENT-FLOWERING
▨ FULL SUN
■ CAN BE CONTAINER-GROWN
■ RELATIVELY DISEASE-FREE

'Rise 'n' Shine'

History: A very worthwhile miniature floribunda bred in the United States in 1978 and still popular to this day.

Description: An upright, bushy miniature, it grows to 45 cm (1½ ft) in height, and has plentiful, mid-green foliage covering the entire plant from spring until winter. The flowers are produced in wonderful clusters, each opening from a perfect, pointed bud to a shapely, double bloom with bright, clear yellow petals. This is a fantastic rose for floral arrangements.

Parentage: 'Little Darling' x 'Yellow Magic'

Other names: 'Golden Meillandina', 'Golden Sunblaze'

Suggested usage: This is a charming small rose for pot or garden, either as a specimen plant or grouped with other yellow-, cream- or apricot-flowering plants. It is healthy and easy to cultivate.

■ RECURRENT-FLOWERING
▨ FULL SUN
■ CAN BE CONTAINER-GROWN
▨ RELATIVELY DISEASE-FREE

'Stars 'n' Stripes'

History: An outstanding American-bred miniature, released to celebrate the US Bicentennial in 1976.

Description: A compact rose shrub, growing to only 30 cm (1 ft) in height, it has an upright, bushy growth habit and a good covering of mid-green foliage. The flowers are very large and showy for a miniature, starting as shapely buds with yellow petals edged in rosy pink, opening to shapely, high-centred blooms that are yellow and red striped – hence the common name.

Parentage: 'Little Chief' x ('Little Darling' x 'Ferdinand Pichard')

Other names: None

Suggested usage: This is a very showy rose for a container, positioned in full sun during the summer. It could be planted in window boxes or as a low hedge.

■ RECURRENT-FLOWERING
▨ FULL SUN
■ CAN BE CONTAINER-GROWN
■ RELATIVELY DISEASE-FREE

'Sweet Chariot'

History: A well-known miniature, introduced into Britain in 1984, and prized for its deep purple-red flowers.

Description: A compact miniature, it grows to 45 cm (1½ ft), and has plentiful, healthy, bright green foliage which acts as a good backdrop for the flowers. The small, tight buds open to small but brightly coloured, fully double blooms that have rich purple-red petals and a distinctive, light fragrance. The flowers are carried in quite large clusters and are good for cutting.

Parentage: Unknown

Other names: None

Suggested usage: 'Sweet Chariot' is a stand-out rose because of its unusual, strong colour. Plant it in a bed of pastel shades so that it really makes a statement, or grow it in a pot in a sunny courtyard for a summer-long display.

- RECURRENT-FLOWERING
- FULL SUN
- CAN BE CONTAINER-GROWN
- RELATIVELY DISEASE-FREE

'The Fairy'

History: A procumbent polyantha rose bred in Britain in 1932, and grown consistently ever since, prized for its perfectly formed, miniature blooms.

Description: This is a wonderful little rose, growing to 1 m (3 ft) or more in height, with plentiful, mid-green, glossy foliage that should remain healthy right through the season in hot, dry climates. The flowers are produced in large, showy trusses, each flower being well formed and double, with clear pink petals that fade to pale pink and then white as they age, while they still hold their shape.

Parentage: 'Paul Crampel' x 'Lady Gay'

Other names: None

Suggested usage: An excellent rose for bedding and mass-planting, it will produce a long-term summer display even in quite harsh climates. It is also sometimes used as a hedge, and can be trimmed back as a groundcover against a sloping bank.

■ RECURRENT-FLOWERING
■ FULL SUN
■ CAN BE CONTAINER-GROWN
■ RELATIVELY DISEASE-FREE

'Top Gear'

History: A distinctive rose, this is one of a series of 'handpainted' blooms developed by the former Irish breeder McGredy in the early 1980s.

Description: Growing to only 35 cm (13¾ in), it is a dainty shrub with a good covering of mid-green, semi-glossy foliage that gives the overall plant a healthy appearance. The flowers are semi-double and open with red petals that have an off-white centre and reverse, and prominent yellow stamens.

Parentage: 'Eyepaint' x 'Ko's Yellow'

Other names: 'Little Artist'

Suggested usage: A charming small rose, it can be grown effectively in a container, making a really pretty display. Group several together at the front of a border for greater impact.

■ RECURRENT-FLOWERING
■ FULL SUN
■ CAN BE CONTAINER-GROWN
■ DISEASE-RESISTANT

Glossary

Alternate Single leaves that emerge from a node on either side of a stem.

Anther The pollen-bearing part of the plant. Usually carried on a filament.

Bare-rooted roses Plants that are sold during the winter with their roots bare and exposed (i.e., they do not come in a container with their roots surrounded by soil). This is an inexpensive and effective way of adding new roses to your collection.

Deadheading The process of removing the fading or dead flowerheads routinely in order to keep the plant tidy and to encourage further blooming in recurrent-flowering varieties.

Disbud The removal of excess flower buds to produce larger blooms. The buds are pinched out by the fingertips.

Dormant The period when no growth of the plant occurs, from late autumn to late winter. This is a good time to transplant roses or to introduce bare-rooted varieties to the garden.

Espalier A method of training a plant against a wall, trellis or some other form of support to produce a formal, structured shape.

Eye The centre of the flower. In some roses it is a highly decorative feature, with a contrasting colour to the petal (e.g., a fan of red petals with a pure white 'eye').

Flush The appearance of the flowers. The first flush generally occurs in late spring.

Graft A propagation technique in which a section of one plant is united with the rootstock of another. The desired variety is on top, providing the display.

Groundcovering roses Low-growing rose varieties that produce long, flowering stems to cover the soil surface.

Hard pruning The process of cutting back the stems to within several nodes of their base. Some varieties, such

as hybrid tea roses, respond well to this technique, while other varieties, especially old-fashioned roses, prefer just a light pruning.

Hardy A term used to describe roses that can withstand extremely cold conditions and even quite severe frosts. In warm climates, this also means that the plants are relatively drought-resistant.

Hedging rose Rose varieties that produce a dense, shrubby bush that is ideal for creating a flowering hedge when mass-planted.

Humus Organic matter, such as compost, which can be used as a soil builder and a fertilizer.

Hybridization The process of cross-pollinating two rose varieties to produce a new and different variety. Many old roses are natural hybrids that simply cross-pollinated in the wild.

Inflorescence A cluster of flowers; also used to describe the disposition of the flower on the floral axis.

Lateral The side growth from a shoot. In climbing roses these are the stems that are eventually pruned back after flowering, rather than the main growing (twining) stems.

Layering A form of propagation in which the growing stem is nicked and inserted into the soil to produce new roots. The section is then removed and transplanted into the ground to form a new plant.

Leaching A situation where nutrients wash away after rainfall or watering, generally in free-draining, sandy soils.

Leggy Plants that have extensive, untidy growth habits. Long stems are often produced that detract from the overall shape and form of the plant. Routine pruning back helps control this characteristic.

Microclimate A sheltered area of the garden that affords protection for more sensitive plants. Good examples include south-facing walls (northern hemisphere) or north-facing walls (southern hemisphere) that increase summer heat; and open areas with good air circulation that reduce humidity and therefore help to control fungal problems such as black spot.

Mulch A thick layer of organic material used to suppress weed growth and prevent the soil from drying out between waterings. Mulches of newspaper and straw are often combined for maximum effect.

Node The point on a stem at the joint of a leaf axil. This is also the point of the stem where the roots develop when a cutting is taken (most cuttings are made just below the leaf node).

Organic matter Soil-building material that is based on previously living or decomposed material (i.e., compost, animal manures and worm castings). It is often rich in nutrients that are capable of feeding plants.

Pillar roses Climbing varieties that produce plenty of lush, flowering side shoots and are therefore ideal for training up a column or pillar to produce a dramatic display.

Procumbent roses Low-growing, spreading rose varieties that are used as a groundcover.

Propagation The act of reproducing plants either vegetatively (from cuttings etc.) or from seed. It can also including grafting and tissue culture.

Ramblers Rose varieties that produce masses of long, arching stems that frequently tangle together to form a huge, shrubby mass. They are more prolific in their stem growth than climbers.

Recurrent-flowering Roses that flower more than once during a growing season. Some flower during late spring to early summer then continue to produce blooms right through until autumn. Others produce a good flush of flowers in late spring to early summer, then a second blooming in autumn. The second flush of flowers is often less prolific.

Rootstock The base and roots of a rose onto which the desired variety has been grafted. Often vigorous rootstocks are used to promote good growth of more delicate varieties.

Rosehip The seed-bearing part of the plant, often presented as a decorative capsule that follows the flowerheads. Not all roses produce hips and, unless they are very decorative (or are being used for propagation purposes), they are best removed to concentrate the vigour of the plant.

Shoots The new growth on the plant; usually the stems that produce the foliage.

Slow release-fertilizer A plant food that leaches nutrients slowly to plants rather than providing them with a sudden burst of fertilizer. Many organic mulches, such as compost and well-rotted animal manures, act as slow-release plant food and are therefore very effective.

Species In the context of roses, these are the original wild form of the plant. They are usually listed with the genus *Rosa* following by the species name, e.g. *Rosa gallica*.

Sport An accidental mutation that sometimes carries different characteristics from the parent plant. This is a popular form of introducing new and unusual varieties.

Stamen The pollen-producing part of the plant, usually consisting of a stalk (filament) and anther. In many older roses these are prominent and therefore a highly decorative feature.

Standard A rose variety that has been grafted onto a slender, medium-sized stem that will create a spectacular display when in flower. There are low, medium and tall standards available at specialist rose nurseries.

Sucker A shoot or stem (often multiple) that emerges from the base of a grafted rose. It can occur if the rootstock is accidentally injured. These are best removed with clean, sharp secateurs as close to the main trunk as possible.

Tender Roses that are susceptible to frosts and low winter temperatures. They are not suitable for colder climates unless given protection from autumn into spring.

Watershoot A vigorous, upright growth that generally appears in summer. These are best removed with clean, sharp secateurs as close to the main trunk of the rose as possible.

Weeping standard A grafted climbing or rambling rose that is carried on a tall, slender stem to produce a canopy of foliage and flowers. It is very useful in flower beds to lift colour from ground level.

Index

First published in 2006 by Murdoch Books Pty Limited

Murdoch Books Pty Limited Australia
Pier 8/9, 23 Hickson Road
Sydney NSW 2000
Phone: 61 (02) 8220 2000
Fax: 61 (02) 8220 2558

Murdoch Books UK Limited
Erico House, 6th Floor North
93/99 Upper Richmond Road
Putney, London SW15 2TG
Phone: + 44 (0) 20 8785 5995
Fax: + 44 (0) 20 8785 5985

www.murdochbooks.com.au

Chief Executive: Juliet Rogers
Publisher: Kay Scarlett

Design Manager: Vivien Valk
Design: Alex Frampton
Editor: Ariana Klepac
Production: Megan Alsop

Photographs: Lorna Rose (except for Mary Moody: pages 23 and 24)

Printed by C & C Offset Printing Co., Ltd.
Printed in China

National Library of Australia Cataloguing-in-Publication Data:
Moody, Mary, 1950– . Mary Moody's roses. Includes index.
ISBN 1 74045 856 7.
ISBN 978 1 74045 856 6.
1. Roses. 2. Rose culture. I. Title. 635.933734

front cover: 'Mme Alfred Carrière', back cover: 'Charles Austin', page 5: 'Redouté'